Dedication:

For James, because you have expectations of me

Give Me To The Moon

Wrap me within cherished blankets, threadbare
a blanket with a distinct smell of home
lay me gently into a bed of flowers
that shelter me from sight
Because this night
has in store for me
a most rare blessing
Gift me to the moon, please
because my time here on earth
has been a time wasted
my echo seeks a creature
of oddities that I possess
and have always guessed
I was alone to have
Gift me to the moon, baby
I desire a place to belong where
songs are sung in my name
and eyes glisten upon my beauty
I will ascend
given to the moon
her majestic self
would welcome me
in my wildest dreams
a shroud upon my shoulders
a blanket
a home forgotten
Gift me to the moon, honey
leave me for the taking
there was no mark I was making

just an echo resounding off
the people who claim to love me
and I, who abused such love
took what I craved and needed
for the consumption of comforts
I've never, ever, deserved
Give me to the moon
as my time here on earth is finished
my spirit has diminished
without a sliver of resonance
I am a vessel unfitting
Give me to the moon, sweetheart
And I'll thank you for the abandonment
my time here was atonement
kiss my cheeks, my forehead
rest yours against mine
and breathe
I was only a memory...

That Snow White

The classic and typical white as snow
but in the depths-- glows
a darkness
that captures young men
turning them into makeshift slaves
ones that mask emotions to behave

she removed their names
their identities wiped
but her- that beauty in the snow
that cloak in the wind
that mind ghosting others like prickly fingertips
that snow, that snow
white,
no not so pure or bright
she thrives on the night
sinking pearly teeth into unsuspecting apples
meant for the good people
that she preys on
that snow, that snow white
lies-- a coward in plain sight
her true nature is obscures
and the only real vision of her
is in the mirror on a snowy mountainside
that she keeps hidden
because if discovered
death would come- bidden

Fuck Me Right

The thing about pleasure
is that, if not satisfactory, there is
a distance between the pleasurer and the pleasured
but I think, in my darker moments,

of the pleasure I steal from you
taking you into doorless rooms
to laugh and joke
put heads together but never, not ever
touch
because touch between us
would be sacrilege
and fuck- would I
suffer in your arms
ever so beautifully
I wish I were a man
the man you needed
wanted
but I am just a woman
and there is no just about it
but I can't help but hate what I am
when I truly feel designed for you
and what I would give
the cutting off of limbs
to get to you
but never could I
make that final connection
and a goodbye is closing in
the tears to be cried
what I would give for you to
fuck me right
the truest of true connections
because I see into you
and I know you see into me
but the meshing of us will never be
because you need the company of the masculine

and I am resolutely feminine
such a juxtaposition strikes me in the face
when I watch your retreating back
and the angles of your jaw
lips pulling away from your teeth into
faces of beautific expression
and I am always, always removed from you
never quite within arms reach
you sequester me safely at a distance
as I will always remain
but if you ever felt an exception to the rules
of you
I would let you fuck me right
because, inside, there must be some mechanism
to release or unlatch
this misery of my unlovability
I just want your love
I just want you to fuck me right
but despite the woes and riddles
I stare into you and
wonder....

---

dichotomy

The nature of me
Is to nurture that which I love
And, somehow, I'm not usually loved

Well or much.
That's quite fine- but no
It isn't because the nature of me is
To grieve
I am less than I was
Do my experiences give me validity
Are my words caressing ears that are disgusted by me
I'd tell you
How I screamed into the phone
The counselor on the other in
Dedicating her time to lost people like me
That I lost a friend
And it's now that I realize
I never had one in you
There's too much taboo
I'm pulled at the wrists
Passes of fleeting fancies
That turn out to be reoccurring
That I wish I could smother
With my favorite pillow
The dichotomy is this
You and him
Encased by my sin
Should never let me in
Don't say my name to the wind
I'll hear it, I'll hear it
I'll believe, I'll believe
And belief is the worse thing in this life
And its best friend hope
Everyone should leave me alone
My pain gnaws me to the bone

That's okay, that's okay
I'm okay, I'm fine, I'm alright
Sobs are normal every night
You and him win
I'll claw at my skin
In attempt
To remove you both
But I know
You're too much like home

I still care

In the midnight hour
I still care
But in the others
I still dare
Under the burning sun
And that longed for moon
To claim you
In some small way
A way only I know
That only I can
And I know I still care
Across time and distance
Because with your existence
My chest is without its void

Its' capacity exceeding
Filled with warmth of a million moons
And in the midnight hour
I still care
It's not fair
No, not when I'm here
And you're there
The sweetness of you
Smarts like a sour candy
Because it only means what I imagine
And in the midnight hour
I lay in frosty covers
Thinking, you could lay by me
Not for the taking
If I could just give you something
That you might want from me
Oceans and seas
Reliving our memories
I still care
I still care
Your silhouette I always stare
The edges composed
Remind me of home
Because homes are people
Not places
In this midnight hour
I aspire to give you something
And what might it be?
If I could peek and see
Into you
It wouldn't matter what I found

Because I live, bound, to you
And, under weights of swords
And any duress
I'd steal the world from its' axis
Gifting it to you flattened
To bloom in your eyes
The earth I see there
Could funnel lives from heavens above
I still care
In the midnight hour
I still care
I still care
If you're listening
Somewhere worldly
And think of possibilities
I am here
With care,
Sincerely,
Me.

Cumulative Grief

smoke billows up from the top of my head
clouding all my senses
filling my bones with dread
that you've died
and I've survived

couldn't save you
couldn't die with you
and how it is fair that I have to go on
without you in this world
but this hasn't even happened
it's my greatest fear
that you die
and I'm still alive
because you have expectations of me
and I'd be sorry to disappoint you
at night, when I cry
you don't console me
your memories that I cling to
only imbue my heart with a cumulative grief
that reminds me of all I've lost
piled on with your loss
and it's for sure that I know
my grief pours from my skin
as I wait for my turn to go.

Vivisepulture

Visceral decisions have echoed
In the one and only chamber
That holds what is most dear
Taste the fear
Test the folds of what's real

Vivisect this body
It is begging for it
Knives and scalpels
Tongue is cut out
Never a mouthful
There was not a dying breath
Or a saving decree
Cold stone
Trickling black sand
It's a time turner
Visceral decisions have followed
On hind legs
Contorting with sinister
Methodologies
Take a bone
Break it clean
Siphon some blood
Drink from the vein of
What is sacred
Loving or not
Loved or not
Visceral decisions were made
The sand has filled up to the breath-point
Hurts, hurts
The cries, the cries
Never alone
But always alone
My name is covered
Under the power of vivisepulture

Only this matters

Impact hits me
Like the weight of oceans
The sea
Frets over my limp body
That has gargled the salt water far too much
To ever recover
And that's what loving you feels like
Oceans that I'd swim
Knowing I'd never get to you
And I would transpire with the knowledge
That it was a loss cause
And I would die in those waters
Never giving up
Until the waves take me as a sacrifice
The last thing on my mind
Will be you and the beauty that you imbue
In all the things that you do
The molten brown eyes
The voice and the messages
Who told me they had expectations
Of me
And I would maybe wonder if dying for you
Would count
How dramatic my claims are
But I know and I'd swear
I jump into waters without care

Because I love you and I always will
That's been my label for four years
Never had it faded
Only elaborated into a grandiose love
I will ever experience
And I despise the oceans between us
But I know, I'd swear
In those waters
Id follow you anywhere.

Run Cried the Crawling

Falling onto asphalt
Bruised knees
And uncertainty
A behemoth lurking
Dark catacombs
Searching
For that faint light
Run!!
I crawl
I'm crawling,
But never fast enough
Gripped, grabbed and thrashed
I scream into the madness

Of monsters and shadows
I ache for everything that has happened
How dare they
How dare you
Who
I can only love
Can only forgive
The greatest of transgressions
I cast you off!
I cringe and writhe under scrutiny
Darkness encompasses and my arms outreach
But I know if you were right in front of me
I'd scream
Run!
And you'd leave me
To the monsters
To save yourself
And I hate that I would never
Want any alternative
Run!
You are worth dying for
Curse you!
But I can't even
Because I'm screaming for you to run
Because I'm a coward
I love you enough to die in your place
But never could I live If death came
and you were erased....

Need Me

I want to give you the world
By whatever means it would take
I lie here arms wound and I'm curled
In on myself
My chest is a void
Fill me
I ache for you incessantly
Taper off the injury
I need you
Please, tighten the tourniquet
I'll bleed out
Don't you see what you do to me?
Please, let me sip the water of you
I'm yearning for sated thirst
Please need me
I will be of use to you
Accept me
And I know that I am worth only
My use
That has been proven true
I'm so cold now
This death is taking too long
Have mercy!
Carve out my chest
Take my beating heart
Sink in your teeth
To steal my life force
To better your luck

And may it be eternal sustenance
Please, kick out my feet
The noose is ready
I want you to need me
Want me
Save me
Actually...it's too late
Just kill me

You left marks

Marks have been left
but no one but me can see them
that's a burden to carry
and a weight that never lessens.
I don't understand why this is me
these feelings are consuming
my life force has weakened
I would be so easy to kill.
I like to think of dying
because the idea of it seems nice
no bills
no one to answer too
but....also no you.
And I don't want to imagine what I would become
in a world where you've ceased to exist
because my identity is formed around loving you

it's not right
and it's unhealthy, I know
you don't have to continue to tell me
I'm a girl in love
and that is a nightmare
when the love is not returned
even worse when you are tolerated
that's me 24/7
no one watches my location!
And I stare at my bedroom ceiling remembering my childhood
when I had glow-in-the-dark stars
and no ideas of a love like this
and how I wish I could go back to that young girl
and shake some sense into her
never love anyone
never!
Because unlovable people like us
are tolerated only
and our time is limited
I would hug her and tell her to never come to this place
but somehow
I fully believe
if I'd never met you
I'd still feel your absence
and so every single fucking day
I close my eyes at night
and whisper
maybe in the next life...

Starlight

You watched me falter
unhearing my screams of betrayal
but no, I'm just selfish
You are imposing on me
Begone!
You were everything and everyone
that I could ever want
but now I've seen you for what you are
Perfection
Like the cosmos
Perfection
Like starlight
gleaming in sync with the moon
who smiles upon me
knowing the sensual secrets I hold
I know what you are
and what you've done
changed me for the better, for the worst
for the fucking hell of it
You probably never say my name
but I chant yours
would wish you well
even if you dealt me a death blow
I do not even know
how you've changed me this way
your dark beckoning eyes

those rows of perfect teeth
lips of sharpness that I crave
Blades and blades
keeping the pain coming in waves
Fuck you, -- oh, I would
The anger pulses in my veins
And I'm casting shadows
because your light shines like stars
and in the shadows, I certainly belong
and fuck you for that
that I cannot want better for myself
that I search for you in every body I let touch me
am I a failure?
Is it my failure that you do not love me?
I don't look up anymore
Stars remind me of you
You watched me falter
you watched me
you left me
and I've never been the same.

Persist

Something has claimed me;
it is only in a nightmare.
While in the waking world, it follows me
the anger and fury mix-- and I'm scared

that this fictional reality could never come to be
because I am terrified of your death
But I will persist
I won't claim grief
but it will claim me
I won't have a choice
and I am enraged by this would-be pain
I am transformed
Desolate with teardrops
scarring my face with their cool wetness
they shame me
but I persist
you left me
in this fake nightmare
never mine were you
and I am haunted by what you do
never am I of any use
to someone as worthy as you
I drift in murky waters,
but I persist
You're gone
but I persist
a day like this
with you dead and I miss
your face and your skin flush with life
and I will persist
because you have expectations of me
and I will persist
despite my fury at your absence
I'm here
I persist

I'm here forever deathless;

Fatality

My fingers have never ghosted
The contours of your angelic beauty
That's for the best but in reflection
It a torturous want
Try as I might to hunt
For love
On the outskirts
You remain in my periphery
Flickers of attraction
The angles of that smooth jaw
Those pearly teeth in rows of perfection
My love for you is law
Never a destination but a sure location
Flowers dead in my arms
Petal drifting to my feet
Swift agony that meets
Me
Floating lazily in a river
My tears have made
Chains bind me
My will has left me bereft
I chase

You retreat from my reach
I laugh and you give a cruel smile
My love has smothered your life
Gone like the extinguishment of a flame
Dear one, loving you is my curse, my flaw
With sure arms, you Id cradle
But I know my love for you will be fatal

Perception

You've been on the edge of my perception
For quite a while
always inviting my smile
with one of your own
I kept a far distance
as you can't possibly be meant for me
and now you are so close
but firmly out of reach
and I don't know how to see
less of you
when you are at the forefront of all my thoughts
and your affection could never be bought
now my heart begins to rot
deep in my chest
because try as I might, I'm not
even close to enough
I have to rectify this travesty

regain some sanctity-
of love
so I can find one who might lift me up
from the depths of a brutal hell
that I've condemned myself to- but
You linger, as always, in my mind- and
you've been on the edge of my perception.

Radiance

We were radiant
And I know that well
Hell awaited my heart
but it was torn in pieces apart
even the devil didn't know where to start
with a heart that was unrecognizable
so I left hell on my heel
with the pieces that would never heal
A beating organ drained of blood
so bright white
true radiance in the sky
maybe stars are hearts
and maybe we were too
I did everything right
loved you despite the indifference
but I need to accept you didn't want this
How could I be angry you don't love me?

How can I want another to touch me?
A confounding confusion casting catastrophic
memories to torture me and all my dreams
It would be so much easier if you did remember me
My white star could never fall apart
and our radiance, god, our radiance
our laughter, god, our smiles and jokes
are more radiant than most know
I want to remember us this way, but
everything has turned to shades of gray.

Create

Burning for it-- I want to create
Bones dancing for it-- I want to make
This passion of twisty treasures untold
Reveals itself to me in the night where--
The moon mocks my lack of beauty with its'--
Smothering glow
And I know
That I am inextricably tied to her
At night she seduces
A pale ghost
I teeter; I cajole
My drifting fingers grab and flicker
I need that moon to create
Because it's at night

Under her gaze
That my brightest mind is awake
So pale and ephemeral
I wonder if I could lick the moon clean of her glow
And somehow know unmeasurable wisdom
Would she welcome or enjoy such a thing--
Or would her majesty toil unsatisfied with
A lackluster attempt from an unbeautiful thing
I am swathed in her
She peeks through my curtains
Spying on me and my nightmares of doom
I guess one thing is certain
I want to fuck the moon.

Prison

    cages fit with a viper's venomous kiss
    wreaking havoc only for the sake of it
    chaos leaves me winded and bothered
    I am nothing but a monster
    this is truer than true
    because I love people who don't love me too
    what could be uglier than that?
    death could be a solace
    that loneliness that I only admit as ink on a page
    that high chin would be my giveaway
    if anyone cared to look

I feel guilty for what I took
a moment in time
a victory that was only in my mind
cages fit with a dominant wish
I imagine you without clothes to fit
in the shower, water skating down soft skin
the abundance of it waters my eyes
You are stunning, coming in my dreams
We meet with a kiss that never could be
I want to be free
But love isn't a decision
and my love for you is my prison

A Gendered Curse

Lies layered with deceit,
of sorts one would hope to meet.
Lies upon that layered bed
where mistresses lie back
to allow for a tryst of betrayal
lies built upon each other
condemned within a regime
that never spoke of its' rules
but ignorance is no excuse
so, dip us in the lake
drenched with distaste
of what a waste and a telling case

of what women are worth
at the detriment of a man's girth
witches make the cakes
never forget that switch
beating the legs of young ladies
that generational pain
will cascade like a food-chain
youngins are so wild
lying little wildebeests
So, spatter our blood on holy steps
hammer down a gauntlet
Take what you dare,
we'd like to disappear
deep into the forests
with the bears.

The Ephemerality of You

come inside, undone with wine
buttons need to be parted
I watch and listen to you whine
thinking, this should have never started
you ask for a drink from the swine
tripping over feet, eyes blackly spotted
I watch with sickly eyes
as you delve deep into days dated
I wish, I wish, I could take you

back to where we never got our start
you disappear from me
that retreating back still feels
like a deserving smack in my face
oh, this is the greatest thing to curse me
nothing would ever top this misery
nor would I have it any other way
our moments are always ephemeral
and that's just fine
I wouldn't have it any other way
You, raw beauty, you;
Oh, all I said is false
simply what I imagine
how you might sweetly talk
to my ear, as we both
indulge in sweet wine
dancing and undoing buttons
hands and fingers ghostin
You, temporary beauty, you
all I said is false, it's false
I'm a heretic and a failure
and I would be for you
to stand upon a pedestal
if only so I could be first in line
to kiss your feet, and wash them
in blessed bath waters.
Oh, you terrible you
always gone too soon
My buttons are closed,
there's no wine here
melancholy music keeps me company

just like your memories
and our what if's
as well as our never kiss
a want so torturous
I waited and I waited
but now I'm praying and praying
for this love to be faded
oh, you ephemeral you...

Down Bad Honey

The down bad sides are sophisticated
and they love to play games
with my mind leaving my cock castrated
except it's only in the metaphorical frame
My identity shaved of all its hair and character
riddled with the uncertainty of knowing the self
I'm down and bad, leaving residue on the steps I creak
seeping into the residual sphere of okayness
I'm okayified to be this identifiable thing that lingers
on peripheries of monstrosity
I'm down so bad, honey, and I know that sinful game
playing it all my life for those graphic gains
take that and fuck it as the only substance
that can satiate your infinite desires and passion
light the candle that the slight wind could blow
and transform into a shattering orgasm

one that changes your life, and destiny
worship the bodies you love with sacrality
Down, bad fingers drifting along the curves of bosoms
I am what you have tasted
It was always me in disguise
you touched what you never knew
you wanted
and I relished in that deception
spying on your form
allowing for the fantasy to take place
in a partial way
I'm down and bad news
taking your attention to abuse
it showers me like a spurting of essence
that would work me over with sexual tension
I am entering the zone of no return
taking your mind and wrapping it into
my own, sealing it in my sepulcher
the tomb of our (my) passions
devour my confessions
I'm down and bad
giving you what you've never had
but you don't want it
that's fine
that's okay
but I want you in the maddest way.

Bigger Than Us

I'm in my bed
naked and alone
maybe lonely
and I miss you
despite the fact
you've never once been here
I'm in my bed
staring at the ceiling
wondering where you are
even though I know you are
with her, in your home together
I'm not even the other woman
there is no us
but I imagine your touch
It's love
maybe cosmic
but still not enough
my love is this unwanted thing
my affections torture my loves
friends who could have been forever
but my heart complicates the uncomplicated
complexifying the normalcy that cascades
like shower water on my back
I'm lying on the couch
listening to sad music
wondering how happy I could make

you, but it's no use,
because my heart runs loose
chasing after you
despite the ring on your finger
that makes me feel so lost
and separated from you
whom I've only been close to in words
and it hurts
that the vows and the positions above
are so much bigger than us.

Partial Reality

Before
Florescent lights shine into my eyes with enough vibrance to hurt. I shield my face from the beams, feeling every ounce of energy in my body surge. A day for a change, a day for an eclipse, a day for everything to stay the same, and a day for nothing to exist…
The voices in my head are banging around and Heaven, my fierce protector, guards the entryway to my void. The void is a thing that only some people have—and no its' not an absence of something, lots of people make that mistake. The void is everything collapsed in on itself, the void allows for us to breathe, the birds to sing, and the rains to pour. The Void knows all, and the sun and moon are it's friends. Together

they form a holy spirit: The Void, The Sun, The Moon all coalesce in kaleidoscopic shades and shapes. A making of a race, a making of the day, a making of all who pray, a making of those who get to stay...

Having a Void is a blessing, they say. I don't disagree, but I call it a weight to carry and a burden to shoulder. Is there beauty in suffering...suffering for the dead, suffering for the things I said, suffering for all the blood that bled, suffering for fighting in that bed...

The voices are hard to listen to sometimes. Not making sense or giving lesson with no morals. Bending over forwards and mismatching its' socks. Both conformity and nonconformity at once. Call is a dichotomy or duality, or nothing and you would still be correct.

The light is killed, and my body is released. Voids are kept in captivity. If everything was inside one vessel, wouldn't you hold it most dear? Voids are here and they are near but never do you hear inside the Void my dear....

I am escorted to another room. I am without sight, but I see. I am without voice, but I speak. My narratives could force tears or form a tornado that ravishes what I disallow. Suddenly I hear a fantastical phrase. It is the Eclipse day. Before I heard the voices, never knowing what they meant, but today is an Eclipse. The Voids are released from Captivity, so say the Gods.

My sight is perfect and my hands smooth with no wrinkles of use. My hair falls in a gendered way, allowing for beauty to grace me in some manner. I have nothing to say to my captors, though I aim to be kept. Voids are the most precious thing you can get.

The Rich own the Voids for they are the real nothing. Fucking a Void, "filling that whoring vessel" is the highlight of the rich. Tarnishing what they perceive as perfect. Only, as a Void, I am everything. I am every rape, every murder, every heinous crime to ever be, that is what I am. So, what is done to me, has been done a trillion times over. Everything can blur, all the words and all the hurt—I assign the blame.

Today is an Eclipse day.

The Sun is high, the moon lying in wait ready to pounce on her, while the Voids celebrate for their union. The sun fucks the moon, the moon fucks the sun, the voids are together as one!

Oh, they voice they raise, today is the day! My fibers become excited, atoms dancing in place, vibrating for the saving of my race.

I hear the joining of the Voids, a collapsing of sound barrier as we are lined up outside. We are offered to the intercourse of the Sun and the Moon. Our sacrifice will let the rich reign for eternity. New Voids will take over, their hearts and minds all fitting like seams in a sweater.

I see the Sun, who I can adore without fear. The burning of my eyes is someone else and this is my duty to serve. The Moon is prancing slowly to her lover, a kiss of burning desire for her to take. My breath bates, heart full of all there is in life.

The Rich line behind each Void. All of us in a line, such divine linear things we are! Across all time the Sun and the Moon demand their flesh, and only the Void have the excess.

The Sun welcomes the Moon into her with a smothering of light. My heart is ripped out. My Void unleashed. Screams and pain, sorrow, and sexual gains. Pillaging of all things! Voids are no more, and their successors scream as all of the universe is spread across ten beings. Sliced open and sewed up! Filled to the brim with essence of life and our corpses lying in that shade, nice and behaved.

And so, the line revolves. The ten of us, our ripped-out hearts, our sacrifice, to turn in the next people to save our race. The Sound barrier seals, and we are left with truly nothing. Past death and life.

We have touched everything there is to touch, a universal consciousness. You can kill our vessels for the purpose of sacrifice, but never can you silence our right to our lives. I feel empty and lonely, the Eclipse day has all but erased me. The Moon says goodbye to the sun, and she burns bright for her new partners. I heard their screams of being reamed with all of existence.

Epilogue

Now

The First Eclipse went like this.

Tomorrow is the first in a thousand years and I have been recycled into a Void.

My name; my story, my debatable insanity. I crawl back. I've been crawling back!

Deep in the Void, I met myself and it was a beautiful thing. I saw how I am seen, I believed in my authenticity. My vessel could feel pleasure and I pleasured myself for the sake of self-love. This was no mirror or illusion, but a face-to-face presence with my worth. I could see the traces of self-hatred and I allowed it to melt away. It's hard to describe how the Eclipse day change my life or why that even matters. I was what I was, and I am what I am. I am both a part of this world and its' opposition. It lives and I've taken my uses from it to

have life. My death, my sacrifice to the Gods, where the Rich cut out my heart and offered it with a hand raised, allowed for forgiveness. It wasn't the Void I crawled to, but myself. This battle of ever knowing who I am or what I will become became evident with the passing of the Eclipse. How inconsequential life is compared to the cosmos.
In the distance, between the sun and the moon, I hear them whisper a promise of perpetuity.

Fragility

My fingertips and hands are shaking
my lips ponder on what to say
my chest has caved, collapsed and ricocheted
off of my glass house that I keep ice cold within
my leg jumps with heightened anxiety
and how I wish you weren't so important
because I linger on you, but I know that you don't
that's okay, but leaves a sour taste
in my heart, and my mouth aches to shout from
mountains and rooftops that you are persistent
inside me and with that knowledge I can
only cherish from afar
that's okay, but leaves me sad fate
for the future
because I consistently love
without permission

and wonder why I am hurt by the decisions
my loves make where I am concerned
and how it tortures
to love but miss a person
right in front of you
who you dream about
and scream about in
nightmares that shatter a sound barrier inside
the chambers which motorizes your miserable life
and oh, how I would trade something precious
for your affection
but what that might be
what you might see
of me
would cast you afar
You are so vibrant and alive
I can never be what you are...

I Promise This

I'll remember this moment
lips and hugs kept closest
shoulders and fingers brushing
I thought it was you I was loving

I promise this
the light of day will not fade

My hands will never close to fists
My love for you will stay

I promise you this
That I will always miss
are never existing kiss
and I will continue to wish

I promise you this
I aim to love with unbreaking rhythms
to sacrifice my freedom
if only for you to have bliss

I will promise this
you are the start
of all that will miss
you are that shining part

jumping off of bridges
bullets and stolen kisses
none of you listen
But I swear, I promise

I'll remember these moments.

Darkness: A Refrain

If I had the power
Of multitudes
My songs would cease to be sour
If I had the power
Of giants
My heartbeat would echo from towers
If I had the power
Of energy and light
It would never work right
Darkness is my life
Pathways and rocks
The unpleasant shocks
Disappointments and wounds
Needing ointments too
It's fine, because
If I had the power
To forget and to forgive
To live on with all of this
I might have the power to lift
Myself out of the dark
It's quiet here
But monsters never sleep
So neither can I
If I had any amount of power
 I just might pull back that dark curtain
But if I do, and all I see
Is a bare wall
What have I learned?
What have I been taught?
It's as if everything I thought
Is worthless if not worth some amount of dollars

No one calls for my love
It's this unwanted monstrous thing
Like a scar in photos
My jaw has been clenched for as long as I can remember
And If I could just please borrow some power
I would shower away all the sorrows
That have piled on and on
Like litres of tears and bottles of cough syrup
Nothing I've ever felt is enough
Give me just a little power
And what I would do would amaze
Give me some power
Give me some power, please I-
I need to regain power on this thin line
But I think you if gave me power
My world would disintegrate
Into a land of grays
But I've always been called to the darker shades....

---

my tearing flesh

without you wholly
my soul in another body
I tremor, tremor I
my soul- my body
you

my sister of blood
removed for the love of a god
straying to the blessed ways
but I remain here in the depraved
how I wish I could obtain some faith
to walk beside you at the gates
but my flesh has been torn
It sears on the pan
without you wholly
my soul in another body
I cry, cry I
please don't hide-
from me
I reside with you in my mind
my sister of the same kind
our heartbeats came from the same mother
I cared for you
I fed you
I listened to each and every sob
I lost sleep, health
for you to only be well
I'd do any of it for infinity
but how can you delete me so significantly?
I want to believe
I want to see what you see
in a loving father above
but I my flesh is tearing, tear my flesh
I cry, I cry
I tremble and shake-
but never do I pray
because that ship sailed away

My sister, my sister, who I would cut an arm off for
who I would kill for
who I would die for
my flesh my flesh- you, you-
abandoned me
I sobbed and wished to die
than be in a world without you
and you are still alive
I am just a sinful lie
that you can't abide by
but you can call when you need something too high
for you to understand
I'll answer, I'll always answer
My tender tearing flesh
so I cry, cry I
and so I danced
in the dark
because that's what's in my heart
because you walk with perceived light
and I worry for when we will say goodbye.

The Painting

Down a very long hallway
stood a person long dead
who had turned to dust
and faded from memory

and yet, and yet

a small bead of hope sprung
my feet moved and my breath with them
to chase
to chase this yearned-for creature
whom I have desperately loved
and hated

I reached the end of the hallway
and found a painting adorning the wall
with such vividness that I almost said, "Hello. I've missed you."
But alas, she is gone without a note
and in her empty home
all that is left of her is paint on a canvas

My shoulders slumped
and that same lonely and gnawing pain resumed
with one last glance at her face
I went back to continue packing up her place
it was when I reached my spot opposite the hall
that I did look back

The painting was gone
and I stared and stared
wishing and wishing
that I didn't care
I wanted her home
but, now, I'll have to love a ghost.

it's too loud here

noise is empty in a filled room
I'm not sure what is more immense
sound- or it's absence
I despise both
But I also crave them-
deeply and in the raw
of myself and my emptiness
I have found nothing in this loudness
It dampens my mood
it challenges my commitments to socialize
to be a person in this dead world
I want to be out there- Alive, so alive
but I'm trapped in chains of self-hatred.
I have imagined the flowers on my grave
if the truth is- I will never be saved
falling on my face
searching for that love of an ace
number one on the high game
a detriment in the low games
and games I do play
devil games
trapped in these devil days
take my veins
I am unable to steady my aim
my shoulders shake with my repressed sobs

I cannot master this loss
of self, of never wanting help, wanting to melt
into a puddle of misery
this misery encapsulates me in a time capsule
It makes sense at the end of the day
the sound, the empty noise, the social gatherings
they all ruminate with my nerves on edge
and I've have decided
it is just too loud here

Pleas of Misery

Dark clouds and seeking vultures
the eagles of my culture
and the pride of my name
all within me cannot be sane
rainy day are not, are not, are not
okay
I'm fine, and I mean that
I am not a mishap
or fun thing to attack
with words of fury
I shout my pleas of tragedy
I shout my pleas of mercy
I shout, and I shout
but no one hears a thing
I am rotting in this space

trembling at the back of this race
because my hurts and problems are always the same
I shout into the void
I shout into the chasm of misfortune
it is without mastery
that I can believe
in a world in which I belong
but never for long
the ghosts and monsters
I am too much like my father
I aim to please
and unbeknownst to me
I shout only pleas of misery

Meetings of Chance

I am a powerful persuader
I have faced my fears and gained XP
for my troubles
Gained a level
Killed X number of monsters
I saw you and you within the same space
I didn't have to hate myself in that meeting
My nightmares were kept at bay
I am not what I was
I have changed how I was made
there is proof in the marks on my skin

of how it hurts when I breathe in
I faced them
but I didn't look for long
I was scared, unprepared
for such a chance meeting
I trembled inwardly
I didn't know who I was
or of what I was made
I hate how the two of you create
such vicious cycles of torture
maybe from the dreams,
maybe from how I screamed
maybe from how you both betrayed me
but alas that was all made up
Both of you have only hurt me with words
a fist would never fall on my face or body
but I still couldn't look too long
so very directly
my dreams may control me
My face, my face
I am here in color
But don't look at me
I am unwell in my being
Your faces, you beautiful people
Haunt me
and it's no one's fault
My face is bare of it's color
pale and the pallor of a new age
I hate the way I was made
I give up on the two of you
I hate the way you glow

and how your names flow
off my lips
it's reminiscent of love
but not enough
I've given up
This chance meeting was too much
I could barely take either gaze
Sometimes I feel like my love is just a waste...

I have wished: A ramble

I have wished for someone
even searched under my bed
in my head,
but there are only monsters there
I'm afraid to sleep,
the night beckons with stinging eyes and heavy sighs
but I'll wake up with cries
songs of solace cannot penetrate these wounds
I would hope for some relief soon,
but I know well that I prevail in the doom,
where flight or fight is my calling
I have wished for someone
in the dark night
in the pouring rain
do I reach and reach
with cold, grasping hands

to people who cannot love me
because I know I will not have to commit?
the question has been posed, but all I can dream about
is someone,
someone who might enjoy my company in nonobligatory
ways
I am who I am
whoever she is
I see ghosts behind closed eyes
I have wished for someone
I have loved, I have loved
I would know if I loved the people I've loved, right?
nothing could trick me into fallacies, no, not with my heart
that is untouchable,
that and my pain.
the two constants of my life
my love and my pain
slicing skin against the grain
I've loved, right?
It isn't false because no one knows
it's not invalidated because I blew it
it was real, right?
but then again,
if it wasn't real,
I won't have to heal
I suppose that's how I know
the ghost in that pain
that follows me home
slides into the covers right with me
sometimes I imagine it even holds me when I cry
and, yes, I cry, sometimes long and hard

sometimes I can't breathe
because all my hurts ascend
and I come crashing down into my body
having been lifted to terrifying heights
this was all real, right?
I've met you and you and him and him, and her, and her
six heartbeats I've loved
six seems such a small number
but if I could hold six beating hearts in my hands
I think I would feel powerful
and I would do right by them
tucking them back into the chests in which they so belong
I would protect them
like no one has protected me
those names
those faces
murdering me in my nightmares
assaulting me within an inch of my life
torturing me by asking for a choice
and god, if I could, I will hope to never know
what my answer might be
who would I save?
How would that be weighed?
by number of kids, or years lived?
by which ones have the most sin?
I withhold judgement and offer myself in exchange,
but no;
I have wished for someone
stung with wasps over and over and over again
I have given up within my mind
but my vessel must live

was my love wasted
was my time a figment
of what am I made?
flesh and bone
blood and soul
i reach inward for that solace
but I've never learned how to comfort myself
nor how to let another do the same
hugs are foreign
the only touch I know is when I occasionally bend over for a POS man
who might fuck me well enough to please me
but in reality
touch starvation is a real thing, and I find myself struggling with that the most
I've always hated myself, I've always been in pain, but I've also always had a touch if I needed it
it's with the loneliness that starvation of sensation gnaws at my composure
I have wished for someone;
but if looking at the data
I weigh those six hearts
and decide who I hurt the most
or who I would pick to save against all hope
even though I have horrors at night
of sexual assault
of chains and bleeding wrists
of those people screaming how they hate me
how they can't stand the sight of me
and oh, how I love to play the martyr
who would save them all

in those dreams I have to wake
and I have to go through the day
pretending that I didn't die by the hands
of people I see all the time
and I have to continue
to breathe
to breathe
because all will be well
and I have to face that life IS a life sentence
and I do not have the right to take that life
in the end, I will have my death
even if I cant cause it
even if I die in my sleep 50 years from now
I will always love them
and hate myself
for no reason other than a toss up
of loving parents or not
I'm so afraid to sleep these days
the thought of my bed gives me the shakes
it's the dawning of the day that I can't take
I sleep on the couch
because the monsters can't fit there with me
and the memories of my bed and what happened there
are not real
reality and fallacy
I don't even know the half of me
and I have a feeling I wouldn't like her
I see no value in personal growth
or building a loving home
all will one day vanish
and no trace of life will ever exist

but I still continue to wish....

---

just as I feared

It's just as I feared
Never blaming anyone but myself
Because the fault is truly mine
Flesh and bone
My body without a home
I've uprooted and scolded my soul
It's just as I feared
I could simply disappear
Rear up ugly and alive
Hang myself up high
Dangling legs and gasping air
I wish I had it in me to care
About myself
Nothing has happened
No tragedy or funeral
I am just a ghost
Lilting in desolation
My feet leaving no prints for any lover to follow
I am not worth how I wallow in pillows
And how I recall these nightmares

As scenes lived
It's just as I feared
My nightmares follow me into the waking world
I am haunted by them
Your faces all distorted
My worst fears exaggerated
You die
You die
You die
You both die
And I have to live despite
My misfortunes are so brittle
Breaking off in my clutches
I have a pain needing eruption
I have to get this out
Or else
It's just as I feared
I'm here
But I wish I wasn't
The mirror shares my likeness
But I've never liked it
The mind is so fucking powerful
Mines gone hostile
Missiles and grenades
Bullets and AK's
Oh they ways in which I can break
It's just as I fucking feared
I can't look in the goddamn mirror
But nothing is ever fucking there

Placebo

I've taken a placebo
It's the only reason for hearing my echo
Deep in twisting mazes of brush
Where I whispered, hush hush
Child, who was me, and I was her
We stared into that ether
Unafraid, but dead inside
I've taken a placebo
And whined it didn't fix me
I take pills exceeding 1000 milligrams
But wonder why I walk around reluctant
To engage with a soul who might
Ghost against my lips
That are chafed and not so warm
Because I am a dead thing
I've taken a placebo
And I wish it would work
Because I cry
I lie
I am justified
In hurting those I love
Just because they've hurt me worse
Because the cuts are a matter of retention
I must atone, as I always known
It's when I'm alone that I ghost myself

And everyone I know
Vilify me
I've taken a placebo
It's actually taken me
My flesh
My tendons of stringy meat
That must have use
I must have use
Otherwise I am abused
By life
Fucked raw and long
Placebo, placebo, placebo
I echo, I echo, I echo
I whisper, I whisper, I whisper
Because screams deafen
Even the most loyal listeners
God, I whisper, to my echo
I can never let go of my placebo's

Fixated

Obsessions can unravel a person
With careful tools you could unlock a new persona
I am not what I was

I have no destination
Your contours, your silhouette, beckons
Baby, I'm fixated
Stuck on those eyes
My breath oh so bated
Baby I'm fixated
Lost in dreams of what might be
You are unraveling my seams
Baby, I'm fixated
Captivate me with eyes dilated
I am yours to command
It's under the well
Not in the tower
Dark and hidden
That's where you dwell
Baby, I'm fixated
Fixated on you
Fixated on what you could do
Fixated on where we could go
Fixated on what you might know
Baby, take me home.

---

living in the extreme

Having been taught how to tie shoes by a neighbor
Having been taught when to hide-or cry

You'd wonder how I ever expected to be a normal person
That's what's expected-normalcy. But no. I am a coward, one
who would scour her flesh, profane it, defile it, if only for a
moment of solace against this onslaught of life.

Give me a moment, I'd say, but maybe I'd be in a board room
with a fancy job and they'd laugh at me, calling my hysterical,
sort of like you did.

This is so unreal, and not at all what I imagined. Impulsivity
may kill me one day. One far or near day I could say goodbye-
good riddance, and goodbye.

I'll never dress very nice. But I would mind waking up
undressed to someone like you. I wonder if what I want is
some to cherish with all my heart or if that's what I want
most in return.

No one has to love me. But I challenge anyone to cherish me.
It's as if, in the wind, there are names and shades of those
I've loved and lost, or never had.

It might surprise you, but I'm partial to blue eyes. Sort of
greenish blue- hued to the reddish coloring of hair, but
its really your stare. Piercing and reducing. As much as I'd like
for you to screw me, as much as it would undo me, I am
falling into you soothing myself with your attention.

This isn't made up- well everything is- but it's real. So surreal, actually.

It is what it is. Some days are terribly long, you know. I must assume you know I pine now. I never thought I'd be in this position, but I can't complain. This is a bed I've made.

You are not something I can chase. Just know if you need it, I would lovingly give you an embrace in the face of the day and reality that I cannot be a soulmate.

I know only how to feel and I deeply do. I overthink and watch live as a viewer not a participant. I resent where I'm from and where I've been. But it just is what it is. Goodnight.

Piles

With fingernails and clothes too tight, I know I have never had the right, to close any gaps in what I want. It's always over there- where I can see but never go, or rather never stay.

It's been this way for as long as I can remember, long ago,

when I used to pray. I do not anymore, because the good in the world is a fabrication, life is only full of lubrication and fucks me on the daily, in backwoods, in alleyways, it will in the fucking grave. Life is what I cannot escape, and that is okay.

I have this rhetoric of deprecation of self- that I know logically has to be false, but my brain, I, convince myself of making excuses for my actions. I am without a form in the mirrors I have in my home. I avoid them and my reflection because she knows that I am a joke. A walking kaleidoscope of fuckery that upfucks the sincerity of life and good wishes.

I want things. As I should, but it is the being told no, it's being told what to do, what to say, how to behave, that I can't withstand. Am I more upset with what happened or that I was simply denied what I wanted?

How did I imagine it would go? Certainly, I was humbled, but laughs were not what I expected. I'm terribly upset, I realize as the days go by, I am a monster undisguised.

I made my bed, I lie in it, and it's simply not what I imagined. Since when did
going after what you wanted plague a person with such uncertainty, ruin something naturally occurring? I've made a clusterfuck of my life, my world, and I need a break.

Whatever. Everyone can go to hell, but don't worry, I'll be there as well.

A Ghost; A Stranger

A Ghost at the dinner table
Eyes of deceit and failure
Barking up the wrong tree
We are strangers in the making
Strangers are who I know
but I never really know
and I'm a ghost
I float in the sky
I fill a river with my cries
It without my identity- that I hide
We are strangers in the making, baby
Strangers are who I know
But I never really let go
and I'm a ghost
Feet never leave impressions
no one ever second guesses
my sweet illicit intentions
A Ghost at the wedding
A Ghost in that far mirror
A stranger in my bedroom
I float down a lazy river
my arms splayed out, dipping in crystal clear water
I am the master of my destruction
Living on the edge of the blade
where all my choices are made

We are strangers in the making
But please, save me
Strangers are who I know
but I never really grow
and I'm just a ghost
leave me alone
so, I might float
to a new universe where the lost souls go
because I've always known
I am a stranger to myself
and I am always a ghost...

Voila

Here I am
My voice, my shout, my raw scream
Hear me
I am desperately reaching
Into fog
I cannot withstand this blindness
This unsure complexity I've found myself in
Here I am
My body, my presence, my cry
Hear me
I dare this of you
I am within the fabrics that you might wear
Sew me into your seams

I want to be loved
Here and now
Stay, don't go into the fog without my firm grasp
I beg of you, see my sincerity
I could plead for reasonability
Alas! You cannot breathe my breath
I will question my unrest
With the harshest of lenses
Shine the brightest and most clean
Criticism of the era that
I have called into order
Or rather, disarray
Allow my audacity
Forgive my nasty transgressions
And ignore my longing glances
While I inevitably imagine what could have been
Here I am
Say my name
I listen to it like I've never heard it before
Even the score
Because I seek to restore
And atone for those diabolical passes
Of questioning affection
Hear me, I beg insistently,
Take pity of me
I will take that pity and scar my soul
As I encroached on sacred grounds within vows
You have a tangible allure
A taste would never be enough
But I seek you to hear me
I am never as free from this affliction of love

Of desire and passion
Unravel this body
Find all those mechanisms
That need attention
Here I am
Am I plagued with invisibility
Do I reek of desperate performativity
That stages some purpose I do not intend
I'm here, I'm here, please
Recognize my hereness
My humanness aches for completion
My shouts my screams are unrelenting
All I can say, and scream hollowly
Is how I wish to love a rarity such as you
This vow, this time, this unexpected longing
Debilitates me in ways unforeseen
Here I am
Here I am
Here I am
See me I beg of you
And beg I must
Because nothing is ever offered
Nothing has been earned and obtained
To truly be mine and relish in that possession
You've freed the bonds
But I remain in attempt to reattach
Because for all I lack I wish you to fill
God, god, I am here
Desperately wanting true validation
I would drift into that fog
If you lost your way in that maze of

Vows and loss
Cherish some facet of me
Perhaps my atonement
Of how I would scar my flesh in any attempt
To rectify my heinous pass of desire
I'm here, I'm here
Here my shouting, my screaming, my whisper
Listen, I beg, I beg
You are within my breaths
I trapped and stole you in my figments
I would suffocate under growing vines
In my lungs
Where my death allows for the growth
Of a beautiful thing
I'm unequivocally here
My fibers bleed hysterically
Presume to know I bleed
For you and what I've done
Allow me this remedy
My atonement is me
My screams are my soul
My desire is my heart
Here I am
Exposed and real
Here I am
Here I am
I'm here
I'm here
Forgive me,
Disaparate me
Believe me

Believe in my immense apology
It's with resentment and anguish
That I realize
I grasp for love
Knowing I cannot receive it
All because I believe
I could never deserve it
I'm here,
Consider my existence
And I will take my leave
You are all I need
Dramatic claims they may seem
But I believe in the power of choice
Of feeling
Of passion
Of owning and exposing the rawness of my desires
God, oh my real god, I'm here
And I wish for you to also be here....

Call Me A Whore

Unwinding broken chains
Of the glossaries I need to behave
I have come from the grave
Doused in gasoline to light my stake

Its with fire that I become clean
Pilfered from sinful use
I am defiled and obscene
But also deeply abused

Shattered windows and golden silhouettes
I am a demon to bequeath
No not a dream
Something far less serene

I lift up my hands
Worshipping the chaosity that binds
Winding hands around forbidden shoulders
Opening my legs like an unbidden whore

I know what I want
I know my aims
I know how I want to be your slave
Take me if even in those chains

Nothing of this is due
I am shrewd and lewd
Masking sadness with promiscuity
I've replaced all my beauty with horror

Horror in the bedroom
Horror at the clock striking noon
Horror with eyes closed
Horror with cum on my nose

Come to bed
We have so much mess to make
I'll be wet as a lake
If only you will stay

Trauma Eyes I Despise

I tried to tell you
Long ago how I felt different
Which I saw reflected in your hues
I'm filled with dread and the blues
The patterns I found
That paved the way for hell
I tried to tell you
How I can't be living by rules
My reality can't be so fucking cruel
Living without you
Is not something I have the will to do
The fact is I was nothing of use
I was nothing to love
I scrubbed my bones to red
My skin has never been my skin
The demons took it
If you die

And I'm somehow still alive
I will soon join you by your side
And maybe our paths will never meet
But I believe in no power above
But I do believe in love
And on the false God, I fucking love you
How you move and how your eyes dance
I'm in a fucking trance
I'm a daughter, a sister, an aunt
But nothing seems to matter
When you're gone and I'm chasing after
Pounding steps
Thumping chest
I could never again rest
My trauma has latched
Grown fangs
That sink into your decaying body
I've had to face the ambiguity of death
Wondering why I've never found depth
In any of my connections
But I heard it once
Out of the blue
And no, not from you,
That I can't be enough
Because there is only trauma to love.

Clean

Filtering through emotions
jumping to rash conclusions
that's me
Jogging in my dreams
Messing up crime scenes
that me
I've created such a maze of vitriol
people suffocate but I've never touched them
my hands are not bloody to the eye
but they are also never clean
I am a dirty being
I wash away the dirt of the day
but in my heart there is so much decay
My filter is clogged
I wade shakily through dense fog
then I crawl, feeling small
I am an ant
please step on me
I am too insignificant to breathe
Don't look at me, I'm dirty
and above all else
I want to be clean
My hands and feet are sliced up
my veins are tied up in bows
controlling me all the way to the elbows
I contort my body to appease the masses
but the masses want me clean!
I can never be clean
My baggage, my bad habits

they are too rooted
I have to pick and prod my skin
I have to cry tears until I'm ashen
Please, I'm dirty
I've committed vulgar crimes
on my body
I've treated it so badly
and it's the only thing I have of me
there was beauty
replaced with horror
I am never clean!
So, don't look at me
I don't want to be seen.

The Isle of the Lost

Shallow is the call
Hollow is the echo
Shadows linger on the periphery
Spine tingling
Unsuspecting, unwelcome visitors
At the Hallow Hall
The call came
The echo went
Sweeping debris from dusty tables
Turning the rations into make shift meals
Not all hear the call

And most do not follow at all
Bend to the Voice you hear
Keep the thoughts of loved ones near
Steady your fear
I am right here
Shallow is the call
Towering tall
Gangly limbs
Scattered snake skins
Bones line our path
The call leads on
The Hallow Hall
Knows all
Where you began
Where you sleep
Where you'll be six feet deep
It isn't until we reach
The Isle of the Lost
That each of us realize
What the call really was
Where it lead
The games in our heads
We journeyed from life
Into death
And shallow is that call
Hollow are these walls
Heart
Mind
Entombed here in this ruin with ivy vines
Limbo
Ether

The Other World
We are moved on
Shallow are our desires
Hollowly are we satiated
Cursed!
We still rightfully existed.

Heavy Under the Moon

Sinking and drinking up
Those whispering spirits
That creek along riverbends
I wish to be one with them
But never could I
Who despises all things good
Because for all my might
And all that I try
I can never be truly good
Digging and panting
Under a moonlight glow
Burying secrets
That are burning my mouth
The dark spoke to me
So I'm digging south
My bent back pointing away from the house
Nails broken and bleeding
My nose dripping

Grass and earth screaming at me
To leave them be
But I am a beast
Everything I carry turns to rot
When my hole is dug
I slip into nothing
And dance to a hymn
Only I can hear
I am one with the ether
I look up one last time
And fall backwards to the earth

Float

I'm used to the way
that your decisions are made
but that's not why I take to the blade
dealt a deal
by a wicked devil
who'd sooner share a shovel
than a kind word
these are devil games
it's almost like I'm in a devil parade
take me from this charade
of mocking smiles
and promises that existence is worthwhile
save me from life

and give me death
that is not a request
I am not heaven sent
you are nothing but
a burning soul
and from me you stole
my safety
tread into these murky waters
let's see which one of us
will float.

Tolerated

Words can hurt when they are said
but nothing is as big and scary
as the silence and the tension it can carry
the child in me
who no one could really see
was a burden to everybody
I was tolerated
my colored pictures
my dance routines
my voice
there are videos
and pictures
but if you look at my eyes
and my face

you see the traces
of my burgeoning hatred
for myself
because my mother couldn't love me
I had to sacrifice my childhood first
because I had kids while I was a kid
my sisters, I hoped, never felt tolerated
by me
because that feeling is the enemy
and the villain is her
who cackles, but cries too
and I read once
that you can have empathy for a parent
as an adult
but as the child you were you can hate them for what they weren't
and I guess as much as I was tolerated
they taught me how to take life and fake it till you make it
but...I haven't made it
I am left behind
and it seems I've only learned is how to be kind
in a world like this what good is something so remiss?
She could never love me like I needed
we were such a mismatched
mother and daughter
and now, just like in the beginning, somehow
we tolerate each other
I learned something from you after all
how to feel small
how to feel like nothing at all
I felt rage bubble

I felt betrayal so raw
and I felt all my self worth crumble
I stumble through life
I tolerate it and
watch it pass me by

---

time capsule

It's come to a pin prick
The tension in my brow
Will not relent
I'm running and climbing over the fence
Trying, failing, to get to you
My jaw will soon give way
My clenching teeth will betray
Slice my tongue
Seal my secrets
The conglomerate of me
Is exhausting, but that's not to gain pity
You see, my parents never finished building me
And thus, they left voids
I must comb and collect pain disguised as coins
I must retain every single thing that has happened to me
Because if I let any of it go
I am less than I was
And that would mean I'm working in the negative
Because I was nothing to begin with

You see, nothing fills the voids like love
I'm such a lover
I give it away for pennies
You see, I have to retain my authenticity
So I build time capsules in my heart
And that's where you are
You filled the void unlike anything
Better than drugs
Better than sex
Better than I ever deserved
And I will love you tomorrow
A month from now
Seven years from now, I will love you
Because I never let anything go
I'm always alone
And my past keeps me company
Sometimes I lie here in my bed
A single tear sheds
My heartbeats echo in my ears, in this silence
It Shatters me
And I could swear, baby, I hear you say my name.

Author notes

if you see this, I'm sorry. letting you go is the hardest thing Ill ever do. if I even can. love you. miss you. and for that I'm sorry.

Sometimes I Love

Sometimes I love
with an unshaking heart
lifting the veil that shields me
from the uncertainty of fondness
That I obsess over obtaining
Sometimes I love
with a blooming smile
having known who you are for a while
I found you there
Hiding amongst all hidden things
I saw the sadness in your eyes
a call for me to come running
and I did
I did.
Soon you stopped meeting me halfway
and if I were to stop running
our mouths would never meet
ever again
and sometimes I love
and it is not enough
no matter how hard I try
or how hard I cry
You remain immovable
and it's a hard lesson to learn
that I could love you all I want
but if you don't want to be loved
then it was doomed from the start
You captured me with that gaze

I fell deeply into your maze
I can still feel the kisses that graze
but you left me here in this way
I will never run on my way
again
and it's no one's fault
our pages were never the same
and sometimes I love
but I am never enough.

Unearthly Love

ethereal lights and blinding smiles
I feel I've know you for more than a while
hate is too bare of a word to express
the lingering emotions
that you've deserted me
left me to the wolves
and I am the leader of the pack
I as good as smack myself across the face
in place of the words you never said
because silences are the worst slights
Fuck you, and how you're so bright
lovable, and sweet, kind and generous
but then you decided I didn't deserve it
having no choice but to believe what I hoped was a lie
How much can I apologize?

I've no idea how to love you
when midnights stretch into months
and I'm gnawed, on the hunt
for a snippet of acknowledgment
you owe me this
it's not fair I'm chained to this earth
When loving you from a distance hurts
you have always blocked out the sun
my dear, unearthly love...

Sometimes I Die

Sometimes I die
wrapped in knots tied
having taken chance
and paid for it
sometimes I think about you and how it all began
then wish I'd died long before meeting a cunning soul like you
who could unravel and wither me so completely
fuck you for that
I'm jarred and shaking
you always did the taking
and I would give and give and give
until I had nothing but skin and bones

and you could even have those!
sometimes I wish I'd died
before meeting a lovely soul like you
winding down every night
I still haven't stricken you from the pages of my mind
that I pilfer through, trying to undo you
fuck you for that
for all I know, you suffer too
but that would be too good to be true
and nothing you could suffer would be due
because I am the one who loves you
you don't need to stall the blue
I tried to steal what wasn't owed
ran with the sweet nothings you whispered
but were only in my perception,
sometimes I hate you
but I always love you
and I pen these writes
blood letting on the page
in some attempt to make
a difference in the pain
but it all remains the same because
I have no one but myself to blame
and fuck you for that.

---

sometimes I am

Sometimes I am left
While that is an understatement
I've realized "I" must make the replacements
No one leaves me
Because I will see it coming
So fast, before you even know you want to leave
But not this time.
Sometimes I sabotage
And I tend to be impulsive
But I refuse to be left
Even though I earned it
And I deserve it
I should have been smarter
Seen the warning sign
How did I not?
Has my intuition failed me?
I left a cheater with hardly a glance back
Unbeknownst to him
I learned he was going to leave
So I left first
No one leaves me
And that isn't a narcissistic tendency
They can't leave me
Because who I am relies on them
Sometimes I am stubborn
Sometimes I am hard to love
listen please, no one can leave me
But somehow, you did
And that is why my life makes no sense
You were the rhyme and reason
And now I'm just sour notes

Not even good enough for a funeral
No one leaves me, but
Sometimes I am left.

---

sometimes I wait

Sometimes I wait
For a dreamy dawny day
When the rain recedes
The beads of dew are shook loose
I wait for the path to MY untold story
This cannot be the whole thing
There must be a plot twist
A gut wrenching tragedy that bleeds
To an unforeseen but predictable victory
And all the suffering was made worth it
Sometimes I wait for a face that I only see in memories
But never my dreams
I've spent so long wanting to forget
Because these traumas hold me so tight
When you see me
I've probably sobbed the night before
Screaming at my bed to love me more
I'm chained there
Sometimes I wait for change
Wondering what the catalyst will be
Never fully understanding that
It must be me

sometimes I hate

sometimes I hate this life
either I slump to the finish line
or I don't make it at all
even sometimes I'm in the wrong race
braving the world is unapproachable
the daunting place of "the world"
erases all of my strength

get your 8 hours
but I'll take 9
which turns to 10 or 11
and when I am given permission to wake
I am sore and aching
the darkness isn't charging me
no, she siphons from me as I sleep

it's up to me to wake
mom always said
I would be bone tired
chores, dishes upon dishes
house of six and I was sick of it
but naps were for the lazy
never mind the 6-4 of the school day

sometimes I could cry
the exhaustion would strike me across the face

like she did, on a strange day
a sibling rivalry beyond what I could take
a little girl wrapped in my arms
but mom knows best
questions are not to tossed in jest

I remember brick fireplaces
and a small body clinging tightly
the slap was hard
my teeth rocked
and her face was so very cold
flight or fight
and I flew

such a hard life for a child
who wanted to be so smart
despite the fact it was ostracizing
and condemning her fate
tears and fears, and nothing sleep would heal
I found myself wondering early
how long do I need to do this for?

and at 13 I learned what suicide was.
but I opted out, for now
because that baby, and all those before and after
need an advocate
and I might not be the best
I show up tired and rarely smile
but I know my sisters pray

I believe in no god

or fear-inducing higher power
but they do
and since I'm sure nothing above listens
I'll be there hidden
omnipresent
to me, they are worth trillions

---

sometimes I

Sometimes I have to leave on a single light
far from my reach
because it is the only thing that can pull me
from my clutching bed
and it lets me go because
it knows I will once again crave the darkness
this kind of give and take hurts more than you'd think
once I extinguish the foreign beacon, and therefore the day
I walk with open arms back to my clinging bed
she welcomes me back
and in the dark
we are in existence;
the day will pry us apart
but this night and like all nights
my bed sings, the darkness croons soft notes, and so
everything I've ever known ceases under the moonlight glow

sometimes

Sometimes I lie in bed in the dark with just the moonlight, and I imagine a higher power descends and gives me a do over.
I ask to keep my memories.
It asks why
Because how else will it be different this time?
How can I make sure to spread more love
How can I make sure I find my thorns
Because above all else I deserve to hurt
And sometimes I like in bed imagining a do over where I change only a little
But I keep the pain
I always keep the pain
And I thought maybe I didn't know where to leave it
Because the past is as untouchable as the future
And sometimes I lie in bed thinking about what could have been
But never once have I imagined my life without my pain
We are that interwoven
She is me
I am her
But yes, I'll take my do over
I think I'd like to collect more thorns.

The Flame is Dancing

Stoking fire of the empire
Of self-doubt wreaks havoc on my house
I've turned inside out
The glossy red blood is exposed
And that it what everyone knows
Tires screeching, eyes beseeching
I am an unmade queen
You diminished me
Cloaked me in a shroud of misery
Where everything I am is unclean
My life wavers
The flavors of my favorite ice cream
Or the bitter taste of tears
Or blood
Can never mean enough to you
I must evolve into something new
I can't just be something to use
Meet me here
Leave secrets at the door
I want to know you more.
I miss you sometimes
Even when you are right next to me
Under the same covers
Wrapped in my welcoming arms
Needing this from you does not make me happy
Neither does it excite me to know you want to be mysterious
Because mysteries are layered with deceit
And sometimes you have eyes that won't meet

You'd never hurt me except with indifference
No longer can you be hidden, baby
You and I are together for the making
Of celebratory love
So, I will love you sooner than late
Please don't let this turn into something we hate

Do Not Look At Me

so long its' been since
I was so angry
you showed your face
smiling plainly
and dropping a bomb that caused a shattering pain
I hate that it hurt, and I hate that it makes me angry
I cried for hours, tossed and turned in a bed that I hate to love
the strength you provided
is erased
you dismissed me like any other case
don't misunderstand- I knew I wasn't special
but I thought, for a small second, we were both committed to my healing
and that was untrue
perhaps I'm much too harsh
but my world feels like it's fallen apart
and it feels like it's all your fault

I fucking hate you right now
and I know that I don't
I loved you pretty well
considered you my bestie
even though you waded through my life- so messy
just how dare you
I'm so confused and my eyes abused
from tears and fears of what is to come without you
tomorrow is the grand day.
365 days that I shouldn't have had, but
because of you I thought I might deserve them
how can I ever validate what you taught me?
What we've been through?
How can you rationalize what you've done?
You took an oath
and now I cry so hard that I choke
If you changed your mind- it would be too late
the trust is entirely erased
and the bed made
I dug the grave for all the memories
and now I must continue to live each day numbly.

This is a Fine Line

The path I've been walking
thinned out, became breakable
and please help, I'm unfolding

losing steam and consciousness
lift me to the sun
white out the past two years
it didn't happen- it wasn't real
and I don't need to heal
but I do.
How could you?
You asked me straight to my face
to trust
to make the journey
and you want to leave not even half way?
What gives you the right?
I hope you see this
and live with it
because the impact you made
pales in comparison to anyone else
even me
this is a betrayal full of malice
you fucking allowed this
god, I'm shaking and crying
nothing is right side up
the edges of the world have disintegrated
and I am not well
The fine line I didn't see
it has caved entirely
and you are gone
which means I have to be strong
all on my own and I'm so fucking terrible at being strong
without anything to stand upon
I shake and I cry
and maybe you are just alright

you don't owe me anything, but
you helped me see that my life was worth living.

In Hindsight

Everything that ever made me strong
is in hindsight
I am left flying in the air without wings to fly
abandonment is a diminishment of the reality of yesterday
You've gone far away
I'm left in disarray
in the mess you made
and I can't forgive
and I can't move on
I just play sad songs
cry along
it doesn't matter
nothing is real
You are simply another thing that has to heal

A Familiar Sound

Scrutiny is my best friend-
stalking the men with me all night long
we're flawless villains who take bodies- fuck any names

But this isn't a fantasy- it's who we are.
Of course, we're liars too. None of that is true. or is it?
I would sooner kill myself than harm anyone else
but I admire the ability to lie
to watch in dire need for a soul to believe a false truth
Me and Scrutiny though,
we throw it back in the bedroom
cross pinkies with me so I know you won't tell a soul
Join me in that room so I can touch where I want to hold
I'd situate you, prim and proper-
we are not sluts for slaughter
underwhelming orgasms with random men is par for the course
feeling so lost that only touch reminds you that you haven't died
last night,
no one had to pry a knife or gun from your hand
you didn't really want to do it
the pain needs to stop
That's why I let scrutiny run the show.
She knows what there is to know before I do.
How can I commit to anyone or anything when I've only been betrayed?
We crossed pinkies too- she and I.
We circle each other but always end up behind each other's backs.
It's exhausting.

One day though, I heard her voice.
And it was a familiar sound.

Tendrils

Don't touch me
and then leave
Don't stop loving me
and stay
Breathless amongst bloodied thorns and glass
You represent a monster from my past
You touch me
and I'm alive
you wipe all tears
and I am breathing clear
The thorns poke and prod
in delicious pricks of hot pain
It's with a vicious smile-
that we play this game
Ducking and rolling
Biting and Chewing
Our minds brace against the same wall
but on opposite sides
You are a tendril of my own creation
Here to watch me spiral in eternal damnation
I'm here in the room adjacent
listening to the judgement call
That bouquet you made of straw
simply a cheaper option than buying me a fucking thong
Can't you just rip open my shirt

pressing so hard it almost hurts
wait- you can let me bend over first
this is what you want
sure- I love it
But I want us to build upon it!
This isn't painting nails type shit
this is real!
I'm an entire person
with a rope dragging behind me
Do you think I have time to play nicely?
Be a man and take me entirely
not just behind closed doors
or in your truck passing stores
Either love me or don't
And don't you dare say
the choice was made for you
Because I gave you that pass
We made a new bargain
You showed who you are again and again
The past is the past
you let it haunt the present
I see it in your eyes
the demons and pain you hide
I've lift some hurts-I know I have
And yet you like to stab with indifference
when a whole new world could be made into existence
It's you and me babe
You're it
I don't want you for the good dick
or the handy hands
I want you for the smiles and the laughter

the tickles and giggles
I want what I feel in a bottle
You could have some in doses while you're gone
give me a chance please
this isn't a false start
we have to make the time we've spent worth something
or it will all fall apart.

Moontalking

Yes, I've been talking to the moon
Living my life like it'll end soon
But trapped in the aftermath of all my pain
I've done nothing and everything for my selfish gain
The moon talks to me
Caresses my bare skin
Peeking through titled blinds
Dust covered vinyl that my dead skin lies upon
I wonder what wonder lies behind
Or beyond this realm of chaos
Limping from porn-like injuries
That were so fucking good receiving
And my screaming wasn't because of the bleeding
I was retreating
Into my self
Finding the parts that could heighten pleasure
Numb the pain

I weave stories of our nightly encounters
My body lilts under your gentle touch
And it's with you I can't get enough
The moon- she understands
My biggest fan
Glowing as peaks form
My tears can cascade like storms
My breath as strong as a tornado
Branding my pain might absolve me
A tortuous penance for the good of it
But closure doesn't seem to come soon
Once again, I'm left talking to the moon

Colors

Eyes closed
Teardrops on my cold nose
Head bent towards my feet
And a sadness I hate to meet
But I have to live on this street

Every day I have to say
Color are just colors
Just the way they are made
Grey is just grey
There are no relative shades!

Red is just red
It is not reminiscent of the blood I bled
It does follow me to bed
And I can't sleep with out the light
I can't close my eyes holding the covers tight

I'm not blue
And I'm breathing
I am not suffocating
I don't need a new day
Take your help to someone who prays

The sun is not my friend
She does not shine the way
Healing is not for what I was made
I belong to the shadows and the shade
Lying in bed I smile but it's just pretend

Love is a death deal made
I would rather claw my way out of a grave
Then relive on the love I gave
Red is red but I'm blue
And a kiss of love is what could return my hue

Playing pretend
Glaring at what I've never been
Sliding into messes of my creation
Having the audacity to play victim
I shake my head and toss my future in the bin

Moontalk

I spend some nights talking to the moon
She's a good listener
Never interrupts
And glows with her answers of tranquility
I tell her the stories of blades and red
So much red, and it's blood, not paint
But I would bathe in it just the same
That's the problem
I. Remain. the. Same.
My lips are stained with the secrets and lies
I shared and kept
You can take one look
And see all that I am is a mess
The moon doesn't agree
But she sees
And she knows
But I think I'm like the moon
I have a light
But it only shows half the time
And just like the moon's of years ago
I look forward and emit a glow…

Monsters

Monsters are not small quiet creatures of darkness. No, they are malicious behemoths of indecision where nothing good can penetrate the weary victims minds, and so they cannot regain vision; they are simply left blind and terrified. Monsters are not friends in disguise, they do not ricochet the nightmares off of your consciousness. Whispers caress the insides of minds, and the victim has no time to decide if they were tricked or if they wanted to descend into monstrosity for the good of their sacrality.

Dreamer

I am a dreamer- one in the sea of confusion where I meet the illusions of myself and decide which ones to kill to find the real me. I am a juxtaposition of limits- of what I can do and what I want to do and what I need to do, and what I absolutely do not want to do. I know that I need to make money, that my whole set of values are nothing unless there are dollar signs in my bank account. I know this- I know it so well that it feels bitter on my tongue just at a remembrance. Time will tell me if I really am a dreamer, or if I've actually been deceiving myself. Wouldn't that be so very funny? That my sweat blood and tears were worth nothing and on the beach of acceptance I have empty hands, having fought a battle of wits with my demons only.

I know well that my demons are my own and no one can see them but me. And, lord, no one can feel them but me...

Haunted

I don't think most people walk around haunted. That's not unique to me- but maybe the way I suffer is. And god do I suffer. My ghosts won't let me go and I know one day I will join them and I will never find my home.
You may think I speak in illogical absolutes, and maybe I do. But I know my roots and they've rotted, and so, I am as haunted as a graveyard and as small as a pin prick of blood that the needle makes. Nothing will lift me from this sentence and I will take the truth with me when I finally go. It's funny to think that of all that I've loved- myself was never one of them.

Embodiment

embody me
I seek a certainty of worth
I tremble and writhe
in a clandestine battle of woes

where I move in throws of ecstasy
touching myself
hoping for some lick of sense
of who I might be
I bend over for a man
taking and giving myself
because I love him
and how he worships me
Embody me
I seek my humanity
my humanness leaks imperfectly
staining the dresses I don't have
making the bed I never move from
It's not fucking real
This is all a charade made to torment
all that I am, and remind me of what I'm not
I cannot absolve my sins
which are greater than I can begin to say
embody me
I seek a love for keeps
trail those fingers over my soft skin
repeat the motions when inside me
touch all those parts that I keep missing
in my selfish act of self pleasure
My knees are not meant for kneeling
But I do for you
and I fucking love it
I am dressed in nothing by my skin
which I cannot find seams or the where I begin
Embody me
I seek humility

let me hide my stark weakness
Allow me to twist in the darkness of my one room
let my tears soak into my weary soul
I am what I've been told
everything I never got
everything I've never done
all brought me to this moment
of clarity
that I will never amount to anything
you can touch me
you can love me
but it will all be for nothing
I don't deserve it
and I'm not worth it
I will never ask you to
Embody me.

Believing in a lie

Secrets scare me, at the dinner table, I wonder how many are held behind the vocal chords of those I love. My mother most of all. Does she make her living siphoning joy and letting loose all those secrets she consumed? I find that when I forget about my mother, I lose all sense of self, and thus I also realize that I've built my identity on her perception of my worth. When she dies- who will I be? When she never looks upon me once more- will I cease to be?

What if she never existed in the first place and we've simply been exchanging life forces and for a while she was her and I was me and then we weren't anything?

I wish I'd never been born- this life is taxing, it's costly, it's everything it shouldn't be. Love is not a solace because it is laced with indecision and deceit. I never want to love again. I am so hard to love. There must be something wrong with me- I damaged my mother in some way, somehow and it is why she cannot treat me with love. The words fall flat- just saying them means nothing.

She makes me feel like nothing. My favorite film- *Millennium Actress* says a beautiful quote. "I hate you more than I can bear, and I love you more than I can bear."

I am in pieces- dropped on the ground without care. And I feel on this in avalanches while I stare into mute space. There is not a place I call home.

Tomorrow or today

The thing about identity, is that just when I have a grasp of it, a tangible hold, it turns to smoke that chokes my essence of self, and once again, I am mystified and as unknowable as I ever was.

It's You

It's you again
I can't say it's nice to see you
I hoped we'd never meet again
Did you stalk me?
Look under the rocked pathways I'd been hiding?
Here, I sit, I am
You hear my voice
but are you listening?
We touch the window pane
and we grieve just the same
It's curious I found you here
I made sure to cut you loose
I left the back door open
unlatched the fence
But still you crept in
Begone!
I can't breathe in
Seeing you walk in my shadows
we must separate entirely
How do I cut it out
I am ashamed I listened to your song
You made me think we belonged
Everything is wrong!
It's dark and weird
The paths are too familiar
I told you not to be here!
Do I need to cry and beg
Or sacrifice all that I've made?

I guess I've simply done a 360, because
It's you again...

Beacon

I found a light
in the desolate darkness
of a god-forsaken life
I found a dear heart
in a world beating with deceit
I found a warrior
in the vastness of space
who met my gaze with grace
who never took too much space
from those under his boots-laced
I found a hero
Interlacing with the debris
I scooped him up
and dusted him off
it's so mad to ponder
that he's been lighting up my sky
while his world was cast in shadows
and the only light
was me.

Lovely

You've been hiding amongst clouds
my thoughts become so loud at the sight of you
and it's true
that your body feels bold under my hands
you are a man
of complexity
I am excited
and beside myself
with the thought of
learning the hidden parts
and I believe in you
from the start.

Heartbroken

What you've done
is the most powerful thing
I've ever experienced
I'm tall and strong
built up with care
you scare me with your
tenacity of goodwill
I bend my ear to your songs
I need to hear it all

What you've done
has transformed me
I am molded from searing gold
lay me out
tear my love from within
take it with you and let this end
What you've done
is instrumental to my status as a human being
my humanness and my character
blaze with strength
I am the woman who loves with a consuming fire
you've inspired my will to live and
climb to your expectations
because I remember
and You remember
that on my death bed
you told me this
you made me promise
you remember
you remember me
you can't have forgotten
and I'm heartbroken to my core
my breaths are sore
what destroys me
is you'll never know what you've done for me.

I Slave

I'm a slave to my depression
in the manic expression

I can be lifted to the heights of normality
but I shy away
because if for even a moment I hesitate
I will invalidate my own pain
and everyone else has done this without shame
I hurt myself to disguise the game
that I am playing with life
we battle
and she has the upper hand
I believe in a mother earth
not a heavenly father
who picks and chooses who to allow into a utopia
I believe in raw sensation
I believe in blood and pain
and I believe in the tears that rain
and soak my sheets
and I fucking believe that when I close my eyes
and I cannot find relief
there is no god.
I have to be my own mother earth
I slave for an ounce of love
I slave for a sliver of understanding
I slave under my own blade
because I have to hurt
I have to know that I am nothing
before I get any ideas of being something
more than I ever was
I have to devolve
there is no room in this cage
so I cannot grow in the space
I slave under my own gaze

I torment myself in her name
and it is without a destination that
I'll slave into our grave.

Eternally Yours

Roses with thorns
are delicate symbols I adore
The two of you form in black and white
You grow to towering heights
pulling out of my lungs
I have hanahaki disease
my broken heart bleeds
pricked with thorns and tears
My worst fears have come alive
I hear silence every night
apart from my heart pulsing with pain
I curl into a ball- ashamed
I can't escape this deadly game
Staying trapped in the lanes-
of flashing morose memories
I used to hear symphonies
with my black rose
and now they'll soon cease to grow
my white roses are pricked with red
my hands bloody and bruised
everything you do

confuses me
Eternity traps me
I'm yours and his
you are pulling me at the wrists
my hanahaki will soon relieve me
trust in this
I'll love you both eternally-
in tragic bliss

Silence

All I hear is silence
I'm a being twisted up inside it
I can't escape it
and I deserve this
All I hear is screams
I wave my hands like a conductor to the themes
My pain is a playable agony
Repenting is a necessity
however, I miss the sounds of the world
I wish being worthy of acknowledgement
It just doesn't make sense
that I weave glory on my path
I stand tall and never hold someone in my thrall
All I have is tears
I scream and twist in my bed
snot and sweat dripping onto my sheets

This is a pain I cannot defeat
I play the tunes
I hear the notes like my beating heart
the thump, thump, thump
lifts me up to heights of euphoria
I see the world of sound before me
but I can never touch it
I'm forever caged in my silences
I wish I could hear a kind word
or a loving melody, but
All I hear is silence.

Quartered

Levers and mechanisms cage me
the look of your faces resurrect me
upon every godforsaken death I inflict upon myself
I need help to rid the two of you
people I've only heard and seen
but never touched
it was still enough to want and love
I curse all the parts of me
My crimes condemn my life
But I don't want the knife
quarter me in a small sparse area of trees
I'll hand you my arms
lift my legs to assist you

it doesn't have to be quick
what good is this if it doesn't hurt?
worse than anything has a right to.
I've lived and used
I gave and saved what I could of myself
but now I have to go
just know, as the two souls I adore
where I go
will be better than here
maybe you would thought I'd go for gibbetting,
but no, I am no martyr
though I wear those colors
I seek silence
I want death and nothing beside it.

Designed For This

The breaking of hearts
It always starts with smiles and laughs
It begins with promises made in sin
I've been designed for this
Every love is unrequited
I continue to love despite this
Because I believe love remedies
The darkest hate
And I have marks to make
I have heart to give

And promises to keep, so I must live
It matters not how my ribs crack open
Or how they splinter into my lungs
It doesn't matter how each breath hurts
Worse than the one before
I'm still here
And I don't see a finish line
So caught up in the journey
But I've forgotten to live
My days bleed
My dreams cease to be
The passions I want to give
Are kept bottled, on the shelf
I imagine a blazing sun causing a melt
Of all my limitations
I'm the last woman at the station
Rationing all my resources
I have shares for each of my loves
But here in the middle of my journey
I float at sea alone
No one is with me
I'll die alone
As well all must
Still, I'd hope to find someone to trust
I've been designed
To never find love
And I believe there is no god above
But if I could write a note to a faceless God
I'd say, please undo what you've made
Because this world hurts too much
I'm tired and what I have is never enough

I would ask where you were when I needed shelter
And I'd beg for a redo
To make all my mistakes right
I want so badly to see with foresight
The future I behold now
But I don't ask any of this
Because gods are unreality
At least for me
I've been designed for this
I'm here and I live
I'll give and give
But deep down
I want to drown
With the voices of my loves
And a fluttering of doves
That my slowing heart makes
And I'd imagine that my extinguishment
Causes earthquakes and tsunamis'
But my death would make the sound
Of a myth
And just like that
I was designed for this

The Power of Sensation

Sometimes I hear symphonies
clashing in waves to my waiting ears
Forevermore, I search for a home of remedies
But, alas, I stand on the edge with my fears

Sometimes I see a kaleidoscope of colors
spinning in unknowable circles of yesterday
Constantly, I attempt to navigate my way
However, I am left in the crowd- A follower

Sometimes I feel a volcano of emotions
they flow and spew
Consistently, taking all my world devotion
Though I am lost, and I don't know who I am; I grew

Sometimes I experience the sensation of hands displayed
they glide and caress the mess of me
Always, but not forever, I am torn from within the seam
Yes, I'm in pieces, and I don't know the way, but I'm here and I stayed

---

Becoming Love

The Moonlight glinting along the edges of you
I'm consumed with the everlasting and dreamy thoughts too
especially when I'm terribly blue
at times I'm overused

and you could cure any illness that befalls me
in the past lovers commiserated with my pain
slaved alongside me
I dream of you saving me with light
and not dark shadows obscuring all the things bright
as I try to fight my way to sunlight
It's strange to think how loving you
could truly help me begin anew.

---

labors of pain

In-between the rays of the sun
I've labored more than enough
Sheltered by a blazing star
I want to know who you are
I don't who I am
But I like the way I feel when you can
Smile or laugh with me more
You have a voice I adore
One like I've never heard before
I could listen till my ears were sore
Then maybe a bit more
I'd like to settle the score
Of falling in love
Of being enough
For a being like you
But I know that isn't true

You are going so many places
And I'm chained to this space
I don't wander far
And you are not meant to be caged
So I'll simply say
Go out there and keep being brave.

Disarming Love

Ripples in sandy hair
an extension of the gentle care
within the features and edges of you
there is a pleasing warmth that wafts
from you to the world
you are kind
and never have I seen or heard a whisper
of anyone's whimper
because I believe you'd never hurt a soul
you're much to alive
and the vibes you give invite me in
I imagine such delicacy between us
a touch of my fingertip on soft glowing skin
a smile inviting a kiss of sincerity
I'd like to bathe you in love
show you how great the human touch
can be
and I'd love to create memories

with you and for us to do something new
each day
Your smile is overwhelming
It's contagious and I'm near afraid of it
because you could convince me of anything
I lose my head
the only thoughts are of caressing yours in bed
at the end of a long day
I wish that was how our days were made
this is new and exciting
but true and blinding
I hope if it happens, I'm enough,
My disarming love.

The Battle of Lust

You are such a lightweight
coming home late
staying awake- all night
you do this despite
the fact that it makes me mad
But something will change tonight
you walk through the door
a quarter past four
but I've been waiting
My body cased in a black leather dress
a single black glove on my right hand

you stumble in, looked delighted by the sight
but this won't be a fun night
for you, at least
I pull you roughly to our room
toss you onto the bed
ripping clothes and making you laugh
what you don't expect is my wrath
that you've finally noticed
I flip you over.
with strength you didn't know I had
but I know this is what you need
One smack and you yelp
"What the hell are you-
Another
and another
And now there are moans
you rub into the bed like a whore
I grab your hair, "Don't you even dare."
My hand turns you red and blue
you're in tears from my abuse
I kneel and place a soft kiss
on each cheek
reaching for sweet syrup I'll drink
you tremble as it drip over the crevice
we've never done this
but I'm desperate for you to learn this lesson
I slowly take you apart
unraveling you from the start
the sounds you make
jolt my heart- and

with just my tongue ghosting your taint
you cum and nearly faint.

Closure

I've discovered the problem
But it's one I can't solve on my own
It takes two to win this war
And I feel I've shed enough blood
I paid my penance
I took what I did and apologized with it
I put my heart and pride on a silver platter aligned
So you could see my sincerity completely fine
It's long past time
For you to acknowledge my crimes
And decide whether several gallons of cries
Is atonement enough
I need closure, please
I can't keep twisting in this atmosphere
Give me anything but silence
Let me show you how you've made me
I'm standing taller because you saved me
You and I were amazing
As delicate as we were
And I know what I deserve
I thought we had respect
And closure is what I need yet
For now your silence is a knife in my bleeding chest.

Boardwalking

I've been slumming it at the boardwalk
Skipping rocks and taking shots
at wildlife
I do this despite, or maybe because of
the shame and the pain that resonates within me
and I am filled to the brim with envy and insecurities
because you are my necessity
I shine and glimmer
for once I am not a sinner
just a girl in love
who would do anything to be enough
I'd climb through muddy tunnels
to free you from capture
I'd slice open any jugular
to save you from a murderer
I think on this atop the boardwalk
and sometimes I talk to myself
but no one else for days upon days
and I forever stay slumming it
on boardwalks to my families dismay
they think I'll walk and cry my way to the grave
maybe I've made a mistake
in loving you
but it's true however blue I become
I know I love you better than anyone

maybe in the ether you'll find my boardwalk
and we can sit for eternity with our joined thoughts.

Just Listen

I dream of us
And we are apart on the boardwalk
You are covered with fog and fear
I am a damsel for you to distress
I'm ready for you to make a mess
Of me, and kill all my pleasant memories
Of us as friends in reality
I am barefoot on splintered wood
The oak of it slices my skin
I wonder if you remembered your shoes
But dreams never make sense
Except this one
I'm drifting closer to the edge
I'm ready to kneel and pledge
Because you are my one and true listener
I speak and you roll it around in your mind
Spit it out in a way that shines
With you I have more beauty
I see it so clearly
My foot slips on damp wood
I peer into the icy waters of the Ohio river
I think it probably wouldn't take long

To really slip away
But I turn and face you
And I'm met with wrath
You ask who do I think I am
And where I'm at
You demand answers for my outlasted presence
Why are you here?
What do I have to do to get rid of you?
You're obsessed, admit it
And I'm disgusted and I feel sorry for you
Nothing about you is worthy of my friendship
Nor apologies
You are selfish and think of no one but yourself
I have someone and you nearly messed it up
And I sway in the wind
You know, I'm sorry.
I'm sorry I ever met someone like you.
You are a mastermind
And this whole time I was so sure you saw
Saw the real me through it all
I thought you were the only one listening
But now I know you've never heard a word I've said
I see surprise and pity on the edges of your face
But you're blurred away
You've come in as storm
Committed your damage
And now I'm left in the debris
With bittersweet memories.

Lowly Creatures

Within the delicate features
Of a delectable creature
Such as you
I am thrown askew
My heart never before used
This way, that I may take
A breadcrumb you leave
And there are so many things I perceive
Like the way you speak your thoughts
With ease
An artist at his easel
I'd buy and memorize any of your creations
Because you and I are two sides
Of a coin so fine
It glint in moonlight
A soothing silver flame
That I must tame
I take the blame for this
Because I've rendered us silent
I've cried, died, come alive, and tried
So hard to understand the why
Why you reside in my garden of devil's
It's where I call home
I am a lowly creature compared to your glory
I'm never at peace, always warring
With my tenacious will
But time will fester me ill

And I'll die here on my forsaken hill

Dripping Red

The smell of your skin
I SAVOR it
Undressed to the sin of it
I am filled with masked AROMA'S
and you implore the most I could ever give
My mother told me I was GLOOMY
and there'd never be anyone to love me
But I show her when I strip onstage
DAZZLING the men as I'm on display
the metal of the cage is not a death deal made
I see you in the dark
you guard my dripping RED heart
while many possess my body
and I hear the sounds of your laughter
imagine the sensation of your tongue
within me, or caressing my EAR
but still, I linger by my empty cage
wondering if I am just too dirty to EMBRACE.

The Finale

Once I met death as an old friend
But we didn't belong together in the end
Now I spin roses as I walk green fields of chaos
And I'm here and I love it

I lost a love long ago
We'd laugh and delve into dark jokes
That begged the realm of sanity
And I was here And I loved it

Once I was judged
By the pain I gave and I bowed my head in shame
But gentle fingers lifted up my chin and said, " live again"
And I was here and I loved it

Once I was lying on my final death bed
And I was waiting for death, my old friend
But it wasn't death I saw then; I met myself in the end
And I was there and I loved it.

Bartering of Hearts

Good Grace
Let me give you my life
I'll slide the currency of love

into your distant hands
And into your eyes
let me fall
so that I don't know who I am at all
caress the deepest parts of me
and I'll barter my heart
Surrendering my soul
for the grace and mercy of yours
I will kneel under your weighted pains
and slave myself to the bone
if you'd only know
that my love persists
no matter the silence
and the disregard
to the melancholic parts
of my anti-thoughts
You walk the edge of them
lingering just enough
to haunt me
you stalk my memories
I'd barter my heart
Just to get rid of you
and your molten brown eyes
You should reside somewhere with sunlight
which isn't by my shoulder
my world is perpetually dark
if I was smart
I'd have bartered my heart
long ago
so that not a soul
could be within me

Still, I think you will always be
where I want to roam
and I imagine you smell just like home
For now, I'll just chase your ghost
the most I can do for you
is to never let you know
my heart was yours moons ago.

Searching For You

My brush sprints across the page
and in the image I create
there is a familiarity
something is known in this space
I've been here before
once, broken, bloody and bruised
My body was put to use
my canvas reflects a stranger
but I've seen her before
perhaps shopping in a store
or on the beach by the shore
maybe she was a Cinderella mopping floors
and I didn't look twice
think to be extra nice
to a nobody on display
in the places I parade

My painting is a mystery that I will solve
I will find her and know it all
Within my search area, I keep it small
She must be close
maybe right under my nose
Her hair a bright auburn
bent nose,
but beautiful hazel eyes
in the painting
she cried
I want to find her supplied
with all the love she needs
I look everywhere for a soul that bleeds
but she evades me
I go home, glance at my painting
think about the girl I was saving
but I failed
and I go to bed,
brushing my hair in the mirror
and then it hits me
I didn't need to go looking
she's been here
and I've been searching too far
It's me and her
and together we are

Give Me Love

Give me love
Because I desire it
one like I've never felt before
because I crave it and more
Give me love
Because I've been searching
under rocks
and behind ticking clocks
while my youth slowly drains
and circles my throat with a tight grip
Give me love,
because I need a kiss of life
Spin me round with warm arms
lift my spirits
to heights of a utopia
where my sorrows are turned to euphoria
Give me love
Because I need it
Give me love
Because I've lost it
Give me love
because I'll treasure it
Give me love,
because I've earned it
Give me love,
Because I have love to give
End my searching
Shine lights of splendor
on my bowed head
so that I may smile
in the light of a new day

Give me love,
So, I may return it always.

Shoots and Ladders

As a child, I bumbled about
falling through more shoots
than finding any gold ladders
I was all but through the thicket
when my compass beamed with bright light
Shouts and Scampers
Released and Tampered
I lay in a puddle of a shoot I did not foresee
and I am back at the very beginning
It's a dark world
and ladders are for the best and brightest
Even holding my lucky compass the tightest
I slump around on bottom levels
I am friends with the vines and tresses
Never will I ever relay a message
that I keep well in my heart
My other half- torn a part
breathes on level nine
Only eight ladders to find
but the rungs are slick
and they spin at every chance
as if they reject me and my name

keeping us separated
on brace of pain
This is how it's been
I take all the shoots
and He's climbed all the ladders
I stumble in the brush
and see the reality of my failures
a ladder, overturned and rusted in rain
He was taking his turn
and ruining mine
I spit and shine the shiny metal
My compass is now my medal
Ladders I climb
And when I reach level nine
There'll be some shoots he'll be sore to find.

A Love Like This

I am a dual person
I am the woman who loves you
And I am the woman who hates you
I am proud of your accomplishments
but also envious of them
When you stand tall, I clap
but behind your back
I am in tears for all that I lack
Your disinterest is a smack in my face

A place of loving eyes
and lingering smiles
A love like this
ends with death
And It can't be you
My bones and blood
would revolt in the loss of your life
I imagine my entire skeleton liquefying
the moment you took your last breath
Beneath my most innocent daydreams
and at the forefront of my nightmares
You. Always. Live.
A world without you is worse than any fate my sleeping
mind can conjure up
I am slumped over in bathrooms
overcome with the emotions you evoke
My mind breathes out of sync with my heart
As such, my chest only feels real around you
A love like this
ends with a death
And I hope it's mine.
I can't say you wouldn't bat an eye
but there would be no tears
with years I would just be a sad thought
if one at all.
You make me feel small
but gargantuan in a flickering of emotions
A love like this
must end.
This pain must be a deadly daydream
Surely, I can't have survived this long

without loss of limb or sepsis
We arched across the sky, but missed
I know you won't see this
But I cry at night because it's only you I miss
To think of how I felt when I first saw you
Dark hair, pale skin, but it was your eyes
within them I saw a pain
a quiet agony
and I knew at once
we were brethren of death
I was committed to seeing the similarities
and you set on avoiding them
A love like this
Transcends.
All my dreams feature you.
I wish there was a way for me to use it
do something that might make all this pain worth it
but I'll stand in the corner, avoiding your eyes
be less than I am, because
A love like this
never ends;

It Matters How This Ends

My life was upended
upon meeting a being like you
who could so easily seduce

everything I have to give
But as it is,
you remain untempted
walking the path of same lovers
I'd never want you to be anything other
than you
But I ask, if there would be a chance
in another life
where we could be more than broken friends
my love is oppressive, I know
Sometimes I'm so sorry I love you
that I curl on the floor of bathrooms
breathing hurts, and my eyes burn
and I wish I could erase ever meeting you
It matters how this ends,
because I may never love again
My defenses are raised
warriors trained to shoot princes and princesses
Your name resonates with me
your eyes follow me in my imagination
and at best, I'm a nuisance
My walls will crumple at your stern words
telling me to stop loving you
But if you could tell me how, I would
If you could rip me to shreds
I would let you gladly
In the end, I think
I would only love you more
and hate myself
It's my fault
As most things are

that you are far
from my touch and love
that my arms will never embrace
you as a good and loved friend
that we will never again share laughs
that in my worst moments
I will always know I ruined us
I try so hard to not imagine
hands on you
the agony that spreads through my body
is burning and true
It matters how this ends
Because some of me has to be left.

I Will Follow You into The Dark

I'm smart, but not.
I walk but never run.
My will constantly rains.
with a heavy sleet
and you, I cannot meet
I see you infinitely
belonging to someone
other than me
I'm walking across the glass
of the past
it's constantly tapping me on the shoulder

but I turn
and nothing is there
it's raining in my house
things are soaked and ruined
beyond repair
I'm scared
take me away
where I can be safe
and you are replaced
with someone I can have
you or I should disappear
You be here
I'll be there
but nothing is here
to feel and be real
I am a fictitious monster
capable and sure to tear
with teeth
meeting the problem headstrong
my arms tangle in blows
with myself
because I am haunted
creeping down in alleys
hiding under covers
my hands bloodied and sore
my apron drips with the essence
of life
and I will kneel despite
the back-breaking pain
that triggers the most insane and
pained behavior

It's dark here
but I watched you walk this way
it may be a trick
and I may be so sadistically sick
but I will follow you into the dark
your life is my spark
this journey that I embark
follows you
because you are the most vital part
of my heart.

Trading Pain

What would you trade pain for?
I am the only monster
Who calls the brethren
To mass
And we rehash all our cruelty
That we've unleashed on our friends
And enemies
We commit the crimes
Do the time
And reside in a space nearly aligned
Bidding our lives
In a pool of cutthroat devil's
Who revel in blood and tears
Who will glut all your fear

In puddle on the ground
And they will have a shovel
Near by
At all times
To dig the graves
For the names the saved
And there you will lay
In a grave unnamed.

All I Ask

If this is my last night alive
Do as I say, please
Hold each other closer each night
Spin tales of my happiness
Shine lights on all the achievements
That I miss
Maybe where I've gone
I might just see them
And I can know that you are just fine
If this is my last night alive
Sing the songs I loved
Bring family to tears of laughter
My beautiful sisters,
All I ask is to cherish one another
Like each day is the last you have
Love again

Build lives with me in the skyline
Sending loving vibes
Into the tears of sadness
You will experience
I'd take all of your pain with me
If I could
If this is my last night with you
Cherish me with hugs and laughter
Spend all of your lives together
Mark the calendar for all the birthdays
Don't be afraid in my absence
Because I've asked to watch over you
Be that whispering voice
Urging each of you to chase
Your daydreams
I'll be there every night
For every heartbreak
Holding your hands through all the aches
Of life
And I will walk with you through all the pain
Never will I let you be alone
If this is my last night alive
Never forget I'm still with you
Until we reunite
On this side.

Malformed or Misaligned

Pretty bottles are scattered around
my body

invited to the parties
I host every night
a singular dose
takes flight
tries to fight despite the
ever-elusive future of healing
I was born malformed
I crossed all my parallels misaligned
there is no divine in my scope
all I have is a branch and a rope
maybe I could eat the length
bask in my choking
or swing from a branch and leap
into a sinking flight of misery
where I am the master and finisher
but also the hero and the villain
I am without definition on most days
and sometimes I play with my mind
try and conjure up something that
really hurts this time
spinning in circles, as a child,
reflected the chaos within my body
the parties started early
and each glance in the mirror I'm reminded
I was born malformed
misaligned from the first time
I ever breathed
my languages are not translatable
and I have given up hope of
communicating one to one
with a peer who doesn't fear me

I am lack-luster
not worth even the shrug of a shoulder
but that's okay, that's fine
I was born malformed and misaligned.

Parasitic

As a human being
I require connections;
those I watch with beckoning
eyes, reside in the net of knowing
where I cage them with needs and wants
I latch on
clinging with suckers and fangs
My head is bowed in shame
taking up a place without my name
I exist in vain
never taking the train
on to the next
because I'm as indecisive as they get
I watch how people around me get upset
with my reluctance to heal
but my identity is woven into my DNA
I can't be a healed person
I see her in the reflection
or feel her in a random smile
but I don't know her

she's a stranger
and I cannot relinquish my shaking hold
of myself
I can't finish this journey
some things aren't meant to be
and I must accept that certainty
without hurting my family
I can get by
hide the pain
and the shame of self-hate
simply by doing what I know to do
My days will be filled with productiveness
If I can do that; I can be happy with it
And stop making my connections so parasitic

Wickedly

I am somebody wicked
Traversing through the thicket
Where enemies and lovers
Run amuck
And I'm just as likely to be sucked
Or fucked
But ultimately I'm simply out of luck
Such a unlucky demise
To lie down in the road and cry
For the times that I died inside

And couldn't pry open my mouth
To advocate for myself
And I'm as wicked as they come
I walk with aims of currency
My wishes and wants are an urgency
And I would watch thousands die certainly
If my path was paved with bright light
And a heavy pocket purse despite
The blood it was drenched in
I'm wicked as sin
Always taking first
And giving last
I'm that brash person at the party
Who watches all the fun only partly
While planning an escape route
I may have a few quick escapes on record
But I'll spell this out for you to discern
I'm evil
And the wicked burn.

Novel

The idea of youth
Perpetuates the idea
That age has meaning
And it's a definer of knowledge gaged
I find my ways as the designer in the landscape

I know how to behave
And am treated with the chances they gave
I'm done being played
I forgave
And I paid what I didn't owe
She filed the curse
Along with a coach purse
To make her the heroine of all the stories
She infiltrated with disease and unease
Victims of narcissistic schemes
Filled to the brim with memories
Of all that remains unachieved
We could all fall dead instantly
And she wouldn't see
Could not believe
That she is filled with monstrosity
Subtle and precise
That never plays nice
And will always put up a fight
I can't abide by this tight
Pain in my chest
And I've never had a good rest
When her voice cackles in background
Laughing at any attempt to be kind
To myself
And I have nothing else
To give her
Or anyone
This may be extreme
And certainly unfairly seen
But I believe in my pain

That she gave
And betrayed me
A being with her only
I could scream out of control
For the time and happiness she stole
But it stays locked in the bottle
Pain from my mother is anything but novel.

Smoke

I'm crawling through smoke and
Dusty charcoaled notes
Lying in the ruble
Of my demise
All thing things I try to hide
Keep stitched up inside
Have decided to flee the coup
And I've had no time to regroup
I've fallen
A villain on my sword
I have no last attempts
Of a final stand
My life's blood
Pools around me
And I think on the reality

Of my failure
To toughen up
Be enough
And touch those dreams
That I have always feared
Down here
The smoke pollutes my lungs
My notes all turn to ash
As I burn, at the stake,
I have comfort knowing
I will finally have a clean slate

The Cost of Misery

There's something spinning inside
A wheel of misery
With outcomes fit for a criminal like me
Who creeps day to day
Filling those nearby with dismay
I'm never okay
I suffer at break-neck pace
Today the world bloomed
With a darkness that suffocated
Me with heavy clouds of crumbling chaos
I can't command my soldiers as the boss
They run rampant with irregularities
That are hindrances of utmost misfortune

I dream of walking the plank
Directly into an active volcano
Where I can simmer in my masterhood of mayhem and remain queen of quests
That harm me in ways most inhumane
I delight in the torture of myself
And have the audacity to ask for help
I wish I was somebody else
And this was all an elaborate dream
Of cruelty
I'm here
And I breathe
But at what cost to me?

Top of the World

All of my blood soaked tears
Paint me as the harbinger
Of desolate devastation
The visceral lacerations
I inflict upon my flesh
Are my penance for
The monstrosity in my veins
That stings as poison
Its symptoms are most severe
Crushing despair
Ripped pieces of tender flesh
Bandages and gauze
Tape and thumping pain

Quicker than my heart beat
It's such a sick fascination
Watching red drip
Onto white counters
It's my super power
It fills me with adrenaline
I could start a war and finish it
The pain makes me a real being
The small sliver of humanness
That I struggle to retain
Colors my dreams with
Half-assed hope of success
Liters of blood could rain down on me
And I'd smile in reverie
Paint red soaked pictures
On pale gaunt skin
Descend into sin
Of a kind
That claims my body
As a tool of my creation
I can bend and break
And slake my lust for blood
With delicate red lines
That shine in yellow fluorescence
The flicker of the lone bulb
Heightens the pleasure
Of my deadly decision
I come around to it
Again and again
Like saying hello to a long lost friend
It was there holding me up

When I first began
And I think it'll be the only thing at the end

Daydreamin'

I daydream like it's my safety
Net, and yet
I'm never fulfilled
My day dreams are escaping
All rationality
I'm nervous and trembling
That everything could fall into place
Without seams
And my heart screams for the reality
Of love and acceptance
I need no heavens or promises
I need belief in myself, and with it
I will tackle the obstacles
Break them apart with explosive words
I want to be sure
I want it to be worth it
But faith has always been tumultuous
For a creature like me
I can't see or touch it
And I live on sensation
My love language is touch
And pillow talk
I seek a contractor
And observer

Who can guide my reaching hands
Steady the frequent tremors
Smile and be my winner
When I fail
Because the road to acceptance
Is wracked with mistakes and self-hate
I can never give myself a break
Something always could have been better
I could be better
My everlasting goal to be a
Better, kinder, smarter person
Is without a destination
I will never be good enough in my eyes
Always waiting for my fortunes to
Come crumbling down to land
At my feet
And I look into the eyes of myself and say this
"Did you really think you'd make it?"

---

martyrdom

Many labels can name me
But ultimately I am without safety
Stalks of green
And muddy shoes
As I run through the maze
Of life

Where strife
Diseases the land
A godly hand beams down
Seeking a being most clean
I run where I can be lonely
The bonds of love are unwelcoming
I belong to the dreadful and dead
My bones are made of lead
And I'm a poison to all
I seem pretty with my exterior
But inside is superior misery
That will burden anyone who looks at me
Just a bit too long
There are no love songs for me
Maybe I have 9 lives
And will have 9 loves
Each to die for
But the tragedy is
I'd die for them gladly

---

dreamscape

There's no escape
Of the desperation
You evoke
Tight hands claim my throat
So I never say what burns

On my tongue
To make it clear
That you are what I fear
White houses
And mounds of money
Fail in comparison
And all of this may not
Control me
But in my dreamscape
You run rampant
Towers of gold
Happiness untold
You are the king on the mountain
And your love would be immeasurable
It is so terribly tangible
Through the ether
That my ties are coming undone
And while there is no sun in dreams
Something far more precious lurks
A future that doesn't hurt
It's within sight
But going there leaves you
And that is something I cannot do

In Plain Sight

I am tackling a gruesome fight
one that just might
cost the price of my soul
I live on time that I stole
and I want a redo
I want to take my knowledge
and put it to different use
I want to consume literature
from a young age
I want to stop my mentality from decay
and erase all the pain
I've suffered
I want to meet you sooner
become tougher
so that I can outlast this dreadful weight
that I cannot escape
and I cannot erase
the haunted crimes I've made
but with a redo
I can save myself
and with your help
I could become something brand new
a voice of reason
a pleasing warmth
pulses from you to me
I believe in our comradery
we light up the sky
holding on tight
but there are no redoes within sight
so maybe we'll have a chance in another life

Sheltered

Shelter me
I am alive unwillingly
My knees are weak
My legs oppress my beating
Heart
Shadowy weighted grief
Beseeches my humanity
Twists and turns
My love for you burns
So bittersweet
A truth I am afraid to meet
I lay in bed unable to speak
Trembling from years of bleak
Misery that chokes any advocation
Of what I deserve
Shelter me, please
I search for love endlessly
Hearts are a heavy burden
And one is too many for me
I want to come apart at the seams
Dreaming of things never meant for me
Cover me with praise
And affection
 Give me the connection
I so desire

Lift me in arms strong and steady
Blind me with light
So I never lose sight
Of you
 You are everything untrue
And I've abused you
Used you far beyond what is due
Shelter me
I live against time
The clock ever-ticks
A slice into my skin
Turning me into a monster
Caked in the riptides of emotions
I can never control
Emotions that weigh on my soul
Shoulders so very heavy
Eyes downcast
A smile that never lasts
I think I know death
We meet in dreams of unreality
He wears black suits
Smiles with a chipped tooth
His gaze a penetrating noose
He runs rampant on the loose
I'm stalked
Just waiting for the invitation
Into the ranks
Of the inhumane
Who take souls
And bathe in blood rain
I know of what I made

Cast from wood, bone and smoke
Each new day
Cleaves my will to live
When I lay on my back
Seeping into a soft bed
My bones feel like lead
Eyes rolled back into dark chaos
Witnessing such vile acts
Of torture
But I am the only one there
And the marks on my skin
Are penance
For what I've done, or yet to do
I know it's death I belong to
My life has a purpose
To die for someone
Save a soul of value
One that shines
I want no part of the divine
It has no place with me
Happiness is a mirage
Of the born- liars
Life is pain
Salt in wounds
Ashes in urns
Graves to mourn
Shelter me
Once more
I am waiting for the time
To become a shrine
Of health and wealth

That makes my sacrifice
Worth everything
And the moment my eyes close
For the last time
I will see only your brown eyes.

Episodic

My disembodiment wafts smoke
channeling pain that makes me choke
and swallow my own bile
it swarms in my gut
every single smile
cuts like glass into my scarred arm
the cold chills it to purple
it aches and pains
the ravaging of my body
is a death deal made
agony makes me its' slave
the slightest attempt to stave-
off the crushing weight
only delays it to another date
I am within the rays
of a burning sun
that will swallow me and all I love
but it will never be enough

because my misery needs company
and there's not one soul that deserves that fate
I wish I hadn't been made
that I wasn't a slave to this life
and all its pain
each breath drains
me entirely
the bolts have come loose
machinery that's been overused
I need a mechanism to unleash
this agonizing part of me
it doesn't belong
I reject it like a bad organ
but who am I without it
My whole identity has been made
on falsehoods of the name she gave
nothing in this life is sane
the mornings are lack luster
and my nights are filled with dreadful dreams of death
I want to fall from heights
soft winds carrying me
to a splat on concrete
the screams of onlookers
will mean nothing and my jollies will have
been got
I don't have the luxury of stopping
the names I save
in my heart
keep it beating
my tenacity is wavering
The top and the bottom are no different

and all the good is circumstantial
it's not real
a placating fabrication
I wasn't made for this
and I want to cease to be
these cages weren't made to hold me
this body is not my home
it's my prison that I walk everyday
searching for the weak spot
to break free
selfishly
I want to be enough
and this is a cycle everyday
every second of my life
I aim for something despite
the knowledge I won't be enough
the wind won't carry me home
it's always a new season
the pilot and finale echoing each other
my life is episodic
nothing remotely changes
and every day I feel more and more toxic
a plague to
everyone I'd die to save
lift me from the grave
save me like I've paid
the price and what I owed
I've been atoning for some crime I've yet to commit
I am not absolved of my sins
though they remain nameless
they leave marks on my skin

setting in the messages of spinning
torture
that I shoulder
and heave on the daily
because there is no saving
me
and I belong to the insanity
of misery
where my episodes repeat
a loop of catastrophe
from which I will never be freed.

Becoming Blue

I'm sinking
Deep into the reaches of misery
And I can't breathe
My stupidity reeks
And travels with me as I
Slink through my mundane life
I let loose one too many secrets
And destroyed my joy- ruthless
I need to pay for this deed
I need to lay on tracks
Decapitate my mind from my slippery heart
Rip out all of my veins
Tie them in a bow and deliver them as

Penance
I am emptying my essence
It's just a trickle
But soon it'll break free
And I will cease to be
I hope death finds me
I'll paint a sign
Draw pretty big letters aligned
In a cross
Because only martyrs die for love lost
I hope someone ties my ankles with
Biting rope
 And drags my bare back
Along broken glass
When I reach the cliff
An angel will save me
And give me a salt bath
I would rather suffer that everyday
Than face this mistake I made
I want the world to end
Because I'm chained in a life sentence
Too many people love me
 And I can't betray them
Though my body longs for relief
 That I cannot even find in my sleep
It's sunk in
That everything is ruined
It was only a matter of time
You were never mine
And nothing taste of pleasure
Food turns to ash

My favorite music sours my ears
I cringe at the thought
Of you turning your back on me
And your silence is a slap in my face
One I deserve
To think that I would give you anything
The sun and the moon
My last breath doesn't come soon
I can't even weep
My misery is too deep
Chilling me to the bone
I want out of my skin
It crawls with regret
My mind is unraveling
I have to be someone else
What I've done is too much
I can't bear a touch
Of kindness when I am such
A creature of mindless
Monstrosity
I must atone with slices of skin
Repent to the devil's voice
I gave in
The high wasn't worth it
And my heart beats unwillingly
I dream of terrible deaths
Where I am left in pieces and heaps
In my mind I climb a tower
Smile to the sky
Close my eyes

And float away
Finally untied

Surrounded

I'm surrounded
by expectations
by demands that I make it
tomorrow holds more things to do
and I have to turn in all things due
money doesn't spawn in my pockets
No matter what I do- I've lost it
the green thumb evades me
I slump to my knees hollow and empty
my dreams supersede me
my mother resents me
and my birth
and it hurts- that I am a one woman show
people toss coins and thorned roses at my feet
my stage act gaining recognition
I am morose with it
Waving hands
disapproving glares
do I have the energy to climb these stairs?
Am I here or there?
Do I have what it takes to make mistakes
and start a brand new day?
How do I discover of what I am made?
My mind strays- caves under scrutiny

Am I seeing reality?
Am I good or bad
and is there even a question of it?
My stage act ends in a murder most malicious
my palms reveal all the evidence
and my crime is most grave
I took what I was and gave it away
no lock and key for me
I live within the breeze
weep for me
like I weep for all
I am a small spark on the sunset
there for a moment
and gone the next
maybe one day I'll learn my lesson
yet.

The Novelty of Me

I was primed for the picking
It's true, I was looking
for someone- maybe anyone-
who might validate that I was lovable
my mother taught me that I wasn't enough
that I could never obtain her unconditional love
her love has always been with conditions
and almost and maybes.

When I met you- I was consumed by
the feeling of being touched
my mother wasn't one for hugs
and my only salvation in the awning abyss
of loneliness-
was you and the feeling of your hands
showing what my body could do.
You opened doors for me
held me when I cried from anxiety
were beside me and gave me a ring
but I was deceived
you wanted to own me
a trophy wife that you could say you "grabbed"
but the trauma you gave me was more than you
a 39-year-old man- living with his mother
who, at 72 years old, stomped her feet like a child
and demanded attention and obedience
if I'm honest- we never stood a chance
I never imagined a wedding day
I never thought about a dress
never dreamed of your face at the end of the aisle
I saw when you thought I was permanent
and you stopped showering
and smelled so bad that I slept in another room
I didn't want to hurt you
because I know what it feels like to hurt
and the look on your face when I finally did
struck me
it wasn't pain, but anger
and you said, "I could say the same thing to you."
me, who showered every other day

me who washed the rag you used for weeks without rinsing
you who had dirt caked between toes and the back of your legs
me who loved you anyway
me who diminished and still stayed
maybe the worst of all
you and her
who let a man live in horrible pain
under the guise that he wished to live at all costs
who couldn't argue otherwise
because he couldn't speak
was confined to a bed
couldn't eat
or even turn over on his own
A man who got money coming in every month
that kept you both housed and fed
and me who took too long to see
that you both were lacking humanity
and he became a triple amputee
I lived in the hospital
in nursing homes
and worked long hours
coming home to a place where I could not even cook a meal
with the only explanation that "the stove would never be clean again"
and thus the stove was off limits
Then you met her at work
it was little things at first
no more opening doors
when going there you had to go and see her
even if we were there to shop

during dinner- if she needed something
it was dire and you have to rush to her aid
and I was left at the table feeling insane
the disrespect on me and my name
when I gave you my body before anyone
and sat with you night after night
wiped your tears and stayed through all my fears
I sat by with hurt in my heart
as everything fell apart
We took a drive and I complained about your psychotic mother
and you screamed so loud that my ears rang
and your hands hit the steering wheel so hard I thought it would break
and I imagined making you mad enough to hit me
All this felt like my fault.
my depression and mood swings
placed all the blame on me
and you changed the password on your phone
that's when I knew
I'd lost you
and not only that
I sat back and watched you stop loving me
and when I saw the message from her
saying you would find someone better
I made the decision to leave first
you told me I'd be back
but I moved 400 miles away
so, I'd never see your face again
but I couldn't let go
and we talked

you cried and begged me to come back
but by the time I was able
I wanted nothing to do with you
you disgusted me
and I was finally free
but it wasn't fair
that I spent two years loving you
and you thought I'd stay because
no one would ever want me used
even though you wanted me to fuck other guys
while you watched
when I was a virgin and tried my best to be "into" what you liked
I think the story of us is
once my novelty wore off
we didn't love each other like I thought

The Confessional of Good and Evil

A smokey spell
A demon from hell
creaking steps
sparkling stars
Together we are
Unable to move far
beyond the altar
of the OMEN-BEGGAR

A broken wine glass

A smear of red on knuckles-brass
Dragging feet
dark secrets to keep
separated by violence
caged in our silence
we owe a debt to
the OMEN-DEVIL

A grave dug deep
A body not asleep
demons amuck
Many souls to suck
carry the dead beyond
only the best make it to dawn
Say a prayer to
the OMEN-SAVER

A dress made of soot
a compress to sooth a bruise
undressing to the nude
a dark dream coming true
spinning in a daze
vomiting through a drug induced haze
All the things wrong and all the things right
give your thanks to the OMEN-FATE

A thousand promises
and a million almosts
A jolt in the veins destroys hope
showered in red rubies
lies catering towards your dreams

Loving without heart
Speaking without thought
Blame the OMEN-TAKER

A blade so poisoned
a tale bloody dark
Arms crossed behind white dresses
heads cocked with questions
demons and liars amassed
Blood flaking to ash
bodies falling with a splash
Place your pain with OMEN-SLAYER

A ripped lace bralette
A pair of lips unsmeared yet
Long tassels of hair
tangled as the lies in the air
take the fingerprints and
the teeth too
a body unnamed has no grave
All good girls know the OMEN-HATER

A very good girl
A brilliant young boy
go all the way
no matter what they say
Bruised thighs
dead eyes
all the undead girls know
the OMEN-KILLER

A brand new day
A mother prays
interlaced hands cuffed
pairs of feet freed
no thank you's
murder is always undue
but with the devil inside you
you are one with the OMEN-TRUTH

A shining white fence
a thousand faces tense
the world was purged
blood and pain kicked the bucket
love and joy amount to nothin
it turned out we needed one with the other
and now humanity is left without the
OMEN-MOTHER

Bewilderment

The soft expanse of new blankets
or sweaters
a touch on a bare shoulder
the sunset of a long day
the moon saying goodnight to the tired sun
leaves falling to be reborn
we are drowned in bewilderment
it is how we understand our humanness
with a child taking its first steps

a birthday cake and melting wax
all was good
all was bad
and we sit under stars
in bewilderment

Omen

I never keep the window open
the cold wind seems like an OMEN
one that I can never acknowledge
one that makes hell a reality
Humanness escapes me when I dream
I toss and turn my seams ripping
my good will displaced
and my strength seeps out from my feet
I retreat into the watched falsehoods
that I return to at each turn of the day
I have to imagine a life full
as I succumb to the everlasting need
for sleep
and I will never be the master of dreams
The cobbled streets I walk across
are road maps to places I've never been
I see death in my dreams
those I've come to love
die horrible deaths
they creep amongst the shadows
my darkened monsters

when I wake, I can't help but feel
like a murderer
How dare I kill the people who mean the most
to me- forgive me please
I have apologized my whole life
for existing
I didn't ask to be here
I would sink back into unknowability
if I only could
When I see a silhouette that looks like you
I know it's an OMEN
they are few and far between
I am persisting
one day you will never appear again
and my world will find a new axis
to spin upon
my breath will bloom with flowers
of a sort that I can claim
as mine
and I've learned that OMENS
are my dearest friends
because they start where they begin
untouched by my wickedest sin.

Find Me

If I find you,
I might be consumed
with pleasure of a new level
My aches and pains
May morph into butterflies
that touch the sky
with feather-like caresses

If I find you,
I might transcend this reality
and shout from a mountain top
that my suffering yielded pleasurable results
and my office is full of apples and Knick knacks
the proper things are in their proper place
and I am saved with grace

If I find you,
I will lose you
and the butterflies will disintegrate
the sky will darken and turn blood red
I will have to shed-
my skin and shake off the excess
it will slump and steam in heaps of humanness

If I find you,
it might be the last thing I do
because love always hurts
and I think it's deserved
I don't know that I could survive-
you
and believe that my death will not be remembered

you will move on to the next
without any rest
so, it's probably best
If you don't find me.

Lethal

He's Lethal
dark hair, penetrating stare
eyes that find every secret
zone in on any weakness
He's lethal
His smile could kill
His silhouette inviting
begging for touch
small waist
pales skin, waiting to be revealed
just a taste would heal
the desire I feel
but he's removed
and I don't belong
I'm not strong enough
to make him happy
I don't have what he needs
and I have to believe
that if I breathed
a piece of what I feel

He would run away in disgust
I'm lethal and not enough

Devil's Snare

Anyone
Can see that my eyes pass
From him to him
ready to begin anew
But I'm never prepared
and I am scared- Of
the inevitable conclusion of lost love
My wavering soul cannot help but
obscure the true nature of unlovability
My pretty exterior- hides the raw
ugliness of me
and the beauty is sacrificial
Everyone who loves me
Stops- realizes the high cost
And when they leave
I'm forever lost
I could lie in a cemetery
hiding from view
and let the moss and vines
take me as their own
My personal Devil's Snare
the thought of slipping away
to another place
that could possibly make-

me worth something
I see your face
behind closed eyes
you continuously reside
in each span of my breath
I haven't been able to get rid of you yet
my life is such a mess
but nothing hurts more than wanting you
I'm colored blue
tune me out
I run the record so well
Play me
I can't tell which me I present to you
Or which one I present to myself
is this hell?
Does my body have worth
or am I a living curse
on the land I try to navigate
and How do I save what's left of my value
Touch me
I'm begging to feel something real
and You hold the power- of
delicate beautiful features- true beauty
on a face I would love to greet
each morning
but it's not morning's I get
no- mourning is what I have
I love you and you don't love me
and that's obscene
Take it from me, please
I can't abide by this call to you

and I can't swim through these tears a moment more
I'm sore and worn to the bone
My home reeks of misery
and no matter how I try to count each of my four blessings
I am left with nothing but arms empty
Sheild me
Like I'm important
Believe in me
Something worth more than our chance meeting
Leave me
to the grave
tame me
I just want to behave
save me because
I don't know how to brave this
anymore.

I See Nothing

My vision is in a tunnel
My whole world unable to funnel
Out into the real world
the one people talk about
and say it's worth a lot
My sight is filled with shades of gray
Bleak and Broken blackness
The dark is akin to me

My brethren of hideous family
I walk with even pace
No destination belongs in this place
The entrance and exit are bricked off
I could break my nails
attempt to claw my way out
This will be my sepulcher
My guttural screams cannot be heard
the creature at my back
soundproofed my chamber of glass
maybe I'm on display
and this is just a fun game
I didn't spawn this creature
It wasn't a choice I made
And it doesn't matter how I behave
Cognitive behavioral therapy
Doesn't have the power to save me
It's so fucking crazy
that I am made incorrectly
and I remain uneasy
in this glass torture chamber
The shine is bullet proof
the condensation of my tears-
drips
it begins to pool at my feet
the water is rising
my pain will eventually kill me
My own sorrow
is my kryptonite
and despite the unfairness
I believe I am to blame for this.

A Voice of Quiet

A voice of quiet
Silence
that says a thousand murmured words
gentle and soothing
they drift into my waiting ears
A voice of quiet
I desire to have it
at all my hard moments
when the day bleeds into misery
and the night suffocates me in loneliness
I can't quit you
I can't regret it
You've taught me so many lessons
A voice of quiet
I close my eyes and reside
in the whispers of silence
a thousand felt emotions
rising and falling within my body
a place of untapped potential
I can't quit you
I don't know that I will ever want too
The quiet silences me
I am treading on icy
waters, not quite frozen
but enough to chill to the bone
I hear the voice of silence

It echoes with my heartbeat
it sings
I can't quit you
And I can't stop wanting you
So, forevermore
I'll let the silence prevent me from
moving on
In this measured silence is
where I belong.

Where's the Coin?

The connection between my mind
and my body
is a mystery
no amount of deliberation
leads to answers
or a better quality of life
And it's as if my thoughts are tied
within thumps of my heartbeats
I had a dream
filled with impossibilities
that left me ashen with tears
my worst fears appeared with gnashing teeth
I reaped what I sowed
I knew I had to pay I what I owed
a creature like me has to buy
happiness
and I've been overdrawn in the account

far longer than I thought I could
but now I hear the whispering beetles
"where's my money?
where's the coin?
Or will you join?"
I shiver at the thought of odorous bodies
creeping across my sleeping body
searching for an entrance
to my temple of shame
"Where's my money?
Where's the coin?
or will you join?"
I have no reprieve
I know I'll not succeed
but the chase they lead
lengthens the rope
until they for once and all
decide to rip it up
my neck on a noose
"The debt is paid!
Your soul remade
this way you'll stay!"

I am The Nothing

I tip toe across chilly tile
My head cocked- I smile

My hair loose on my bare back
the night is simmering with black

the moon awakens the deathly ill
I think of how much I want to spill
my own blood
bathe in enough

that my skin slips and slides
glides over the goosebumps as I chill
from blood loss
such a small cost

to see my world disappear
there isn't an ounce of fear
I can almost hear

the hounds of hell circling
I am here for the taking
my nightmares are waking
shaking with anticipation

of a new soul
to devour
I ascend the tower
Bare and dripping red
I'm going to my death bed

―――――――――――――――――――

Please

Please,
release me
from this dreadful love
of you
and everything that you do
I hate how it consumes
me and lashes my back
with ferocity
flaps of skin
hanging in the wind
strike me
I need to hurt on the outside
because inside I am raw
and abused
not fit for use
by anyone else
and I know that I am hard to love
that I could never be enough for you
or anyone else
I don't want to be myself
anymore
and I cannot accept that my life
is worth anything at all
that there is no monetary value
in any part of me
I can't see
the worth I might have had
once a upon a time
maybe I shined

in the golden sunlight
but my back is bent
bleeding in clots of misery
I am not good for anything
and I am ashamed
that I love you
when you are not mine to love
so, I will continue to ask you
where you can't hear to agree
release me,
Please.

Anger

I am filled with the most
diabolical rage
I feel like I'm trapped onstage
bet on like horses in a race
what will make me finally snap
and erase all that I've amounted to yet
I'm more than upset
that you don't care
that you meet my stare
with staggering pity
I almost can't look at you directly
because all my failures
all my not-good-enoughs

are too loud to bear
and I wish I didn't care
and that I didn't want you near
so, I could move the hair from your face
so that I could trace the contours of your cheeks
And I could erase the most painful parts of you
undo all that would ever harm you
I am angry
that none of that will ever be true
and I can't escape wishing that you
would want me too
that I would be the dark star to your golden
the echo to your voice
that it wouldn't even be a choice
to make
and you would never look upon me with distaste
when I'm at your feet begging for your grace
I can never decide if what I want is space
or to see you everyday
and I'm angry
that I ask the question day after day
week after fucking week
and there are never any goddamn answers to see
no matter how hard I seek
for them and contort my mind and body
to appease the agony that traps me
in a vise grip
I am unbound with it
I hate the lack of control
I hate that I love you more than my soul

and I hate that I am filled with
the most miserable sadness.

Under the Influence

I don't know what you did
to undo the center of me
where everything I am and do
comes from
and I don't know how
you untethered my anchor
that kept me adhered to the line
of this life
and why all my life
I've wanted to say goodbye
I don't know what you did
to make me hate love
maybe because I am a succubus
and I require too much
maybe I need to feed
and relish in having tasted
you
but I never knew why you
what makes you special
in my eyes
what makes me cry every night
that I am not beside you

why do your eyes shine the brightest
and for fucks sake
why will your face never unplaster itself
from behind my eyelids
an everlasting portrait of the golden star
that you are
I never knew that you would unscrew
the linear ridge of my wavering sanity
I cannot stand to be near or far from you
the distances feel like my wrists are stretching
far beyond their scope
I cannot stand the desolate hope
when there is none
and I am miserable
and you are okay
you are loved
and I'm left astray
You are married
and I am wishing to be carried
far away where you don't exist
and the only time I remember this
is when the world ends
and the sun swallows us all
I think when I die
the last thing I want to see
is your face
your penetrating gaze
under it- I am safe
Under your influence
I've been sentenced
to dire and bleak torture

the outlook is not promising
and I'm not one for compromising
you can hack away if you need too
Just remove the parts that love you
Before I try to.

Without Fear

Your eyes are the blue of the sea
I hope you believe in your beauty
Because I've seen it truly
and there is no one who knew me
better than you
I am used
to the sunny features
on your face
a place of stunning glory
and an unfinished story
You write the path
Master and creator in unison
Your hands glide over the map
None are so glad
as you, who grew
a being so perfect
she transcends all before this
she could never be anything but beautiful
because of the beauty within you

I know this to be true
because I've seen what you do
rising before the sun
saying goodnight to the moon
pumping life into the precious creature
that brought to you so many features
of yourself
never before known
you've grown
I no longer see a princess in tears
or a girl frightened with fear
I see a woman blooming
into a goddess
and she walks with a back straight
she shows up every single day
to protect and fight
for her pride and joy
and I know it's worth it to you
I see it in your face when you look at her in awe
and the woman you are now?
She wears a fucking crown.

Behave

I pull you
roughly onto the bed
you lie limp

and I do what I like
beginning with my face
between your thighs
finding all those secrets
that reside
in the sensitive places
my finger traces
the rounded toys
and when you try to sit up
I say lay back and enjoy
the length of you slides
with practiced ease
down my throat
I might just be the G.O.A.T
they way you whine
pumping hips erratically
fists clutching in the bedsheets
"I can't take it, please"
but it doesn't matter what you say
you will release
as many times as I need
You let out a near scream
and salty ropes hit the back of my tongue
down to the base
my lips slide
you toss and turn
but you'll never escape
and I'll teach you to behave.

———————————————

You Made Me Wait

You made me wait
which, for you, is very brave
to face my wrath
of ecstasy
where you belong to me
and do what I say indefinitely
You made me wait
which was a mistake
because now
I will satiate
you until you pass the point of your orgasmic bliss
You made me wait
a very stupid way to make-
me shower you with attention
You come through the door- dripping
I trail a finger along the curve of your spine
whispering you're mine
no one can save you this time
my body molds to yours
taking you in hand
my position behind you, oppressive
and this is the best way to get the message
across- that you would do well
to lay your head back
on my shoulder
as I place a kiss on your pulse point
your legs quake
you're so close

but you can't take
my sinful touch for much longer
I jerk you nearly raw
you squirm in my thrall
of desire
slick with sweat
your knees give out
and you cum in ropes
I let you drop
right into your mess
and believe we aren't even finished yet.

Always

I'm always waiting
maybe for a chance meeting
or for someone to save me
I'm always hiding
shelving away the parts that
leave me vulnerable
if on display
I'm ashamed to love myself
lest someone pull the rug
out from under me
and I am seen
and I believe
there is nothing worthy

inside me
and the moment I feel any sense of safety
I will have betrayed me
the wall will never crumble
I reinforce it
with harsh words
about myself
I'm in a freezing hell
where I can see the path
stretching before me
I could run and leap
for that lit opening
but my feet are trapped
in an icy cage
that the depths of my being
cannot erase
I know, if I'm at the bottom
I'm safe
and nothing worse can befall me
I could die a million deaths
but nothing would be surprising
down in the rubble
I recognize the familiar misery
I am always waiting
for the day I have to courage to
climb to a better place
where I belong
and there is not a trace
of the monster at my back
but I will be waiting a long time
for that.

The Loneliest

I've been breaking
apart
I can see an abyss opening
in the cracks of my skin
I watch as I begin
to unravel
and I will channel my lasting desires
to build me up higher
the chinks and chasms
Frighten me
I'm here withstanding
the rain and the heat
almost begging for some relief
my hair sopping wet
but just wait
the pain hasn't even started yet
I can't stand here and be less
but it's okay for me to undress
make that make sense
While I continue my ascent
my parts fly off
I'm like a highway
filled with tires and scraps of metal
I blow away in the wind
for someone to look at and

wonder who I am
I falter in my steps
a computer failing
my code is not up to date
rest assure, it was always too late
I need no tears
I ask for no prayers
I will continue on
Losing bits along the way
It just occurred to me today
that for me, lately, has been
The Loneliest.

You Are

An everchanging set of wants
That have existed within me
Even when I think I deserve nothing
I save a bit I think I do
Even when I think I don't want anything
I save a bit I would love to have
Sometimes it's a feeling
Other times a materialistic thing
But most often it's someone;
I've loved
I've lost
But never have I breathed so easy

as with you
I've had joy ripped from me
I've had suffering etched into my bones
But never have I been so settled
Than with you
I steal these good things from you
I hope you don't mind too much
But you should know
That even when I'm sinking
I think of you so I can be strong
The center of my strength has always been
My ability to love others
and loved,
You Are.

Acknowledgements:

My four beautiful sisters, Destiny, Savannah, Ava and Zoe are the joy of my life and the reason I do anything, so thanking them is essential. My school and professors who are a constant support of validation and hope. I am thankful to Karen Trotter, who once told me I was a flower yet to bloom. Thank you. I am thankful to Candi Moore, who taught me how to advocate for myself even when it is the hardest choice. I am unbelievably thankful for my high school teacher Christy Mowery who instilled my love for writing and provided endless support for my creative pursuits. I am thankful for my friends who read my poetry and say it's good (even when it's not). Shawn W., Diane P., Kira Y., and Erica R. are incredible supports for me, and I thank you all. Amara E who built up my self-worth with genuine care and belief- I thank you.

Made in the USA
Columbia, SC
01 November 2024